The Entrepreneurship of Sustainable High-Growth Firms

This book develops a comprehensive theoretical and empirical framework explaining how entrepreneurial ecosystems (EEs) influence firms' sustainable high growth (SHG). Its core objective is to conceptualize SHG as a key outcome of entrepreneurial ecosystems and to empirically verify whether, and through which mechanisms, ecosystems foster sustainable firm expansion.

The theoretical part is based on a narrative literature review covering entrepreneurial ecosystems, firm growth, and growth determinants. It integrates ecosystem thinking with firm-level perspectives, including the resource-based view, and advances theory by defining the output of EEs as sustainable high-growth entrepreneurship – growth that combines size dynamics, profitability, and social benefits.

Methodologically, this book makes a strong contribution by applying a quantitative, large-scale approach that remains rare in EE research. Using firm-level microdata for over 43,000 enterprises and regional data for Polish ecosystems from 2018 to 2022, it employs panel logistic regression, marginal effects analysis, Bayesian regression, and spectral clustering. Entrepreneurial ecosystems are operationalized through six dimensions, and the study also captures firm heterogeneity, prior growth, and spatial interactions between neighboring ecosystems.

Practically, the findings offer valuable insights for policymakers and regional development practitioners. By identifying ecosystem configurations most conducive to SHG, this book provides evidence-based guidance for designing targeted entrepreneurship and regional policies that promote productive, sustainable firm growth.

Sławomir Konopa, Ph.D., is an Assistant Professor of Economics at the Warsaw University of Life Sciences, Poland, and an affiliate at Indiana University Bloomington, Ostrom Workshop, United States. He earned his Ph.D. in Economics and Finance with honors from the Jagiellonian University, Poland. He is also pursuing a master's degree in Accounting and Financial Management at Jagiellonian University. During his studies, he deepened his knowledge of economics at leading institutions including Harvard University, Massachusetts Institute of Technology, University of Oxford, and Paris and Barcelona Schools of Economics. He has received multiple scholarships for academic excellence, and his master's thesis won first place in a national competition for the best thesis in the field of entrepreneurship, organized by the Council for Entrepreneurship at the Office of the President of the Republic of Poland. His research interests focus on entrepreneurship and sustainable development.

Marta Gancarczyk is a Full Professor and Head of the Department of Finance and International Economics at the Institute of Economics, Finance and Management, Jagiellonian University, Krakow, Poland. She holds her Ph.D. in Management Science from the University of Lodz, Poland; the Habilitated Ph.D. in Economics from Krakow University of Economics, Poland; and the Professor's title based on the recommendation from the Polish Council of Excellence. Her research, publication, and consulting activities focus on entrepreneurship, industrial clusters, firm growth, regional and innovation policies, and public policy for small and medium-sized enterprises.

Routledge Studies in Central and Eastern European Business and Economics

Drawing together cutting-edge research from across the region, this series presents monographs, edited volumes, and 'shortform' books on the full range of issues, themes, and topics in Business and Economics pertaining to Central and Eastern Europe (CEE).

The Digital Transformation of Production and Operations Management
Energy Systems, Manufacturing, and Sustainability
Radosław Miśkiewicz

Leadership, Management and Organizational Culture
The Insurance Industry
Magdalena Kraczla and Sławomir Króliczek

Social Media, Ethics and Management
Strategy and Organizational Resilience
Sandra Grabowska, Roksana Poloczek, Sebastian Saniuk

Brand Loyalty and Consumer Behavior
Generation Z in Central and Eastern Europe
Elwira Gross-Gniot, Maciej Dębski and Ewa Szkudlarek

The Entrepreneurship of Sustainable High-Growth Firms
Frameworks, Evidence, and Policy Insights
Sławomir Konopa and Marta Gancarczyk

https://www.routledge.com/Routledge-Studies-in-Central-and-Eastern-European-Business-and-Economics/book-series/RSCEEBE

The Entrepreneurship of Sustainable High-Growth Firms

Frameworks, Evidence, and Policy Insights

Sławomir Konopa and Marta Gancarczyk

Routledge
Taylor & Francis Group
NEW YORK AND LONDON

First published 2026
by Routledge
605 Third Avenue, New York, NY 10158

and by Routledge
4 Park Square, Milton Park, Abingdon, Oxon, OX14 4RN

Routledge is an imprint of the Taylor & Francis Group, an informa business

ISBN: 978-1-041-23953-6 (hbk)
ISBN: 978-1-041-23955-0 (pbk)
ISBN: 978-1-003-73933-3 (ebk)

DOI: 10.4324/9781003739333

Typeset in Times New Roman
by codeMantra

Contents

Figures

Tables

Acknowledgments

The authors would like to extend their sincere thanks to the anonymous reviewers of their book proposal to Routledge, who greatly supported them with both expertise and insightful evaluations. This research could not have been disseminated without the highly professional help, friendly advice, and excellent collaboration with Brianna Ascher, the Routledge Editor of this monograph, and Jessica Rech, Editorial Assistant at Routledge.

We gratefully acknowledge funding from the Priority Research Area "Society of the Future" under the Program "Excellence Initiative – Research University" at the Jagiellonian University in Krakow that enabled the publication of this book in an open-access format.

Introduction

At the microeconomic level, firm growth is considered one of the conditions for long-term survival and return on investment. Growth represents an increase in firm size and is captured in quantitative terms through variables such as revenues, employment, asset value, market share, or level of diversification (Davidsson, 2006; Gancarczyk, 2017). The macroeconomic importance of this phenomenon stems mainly from the activities of high-growth firms, which significantly expand their operations within a short period of time. Despite their small share in the population, high-growth firms contribute substantially to new jobs, innovation, and value added (Birch, 1987; Brnjas et al., 2015; Solmon, 2019).

Research conducted since the 1980s on resource-based determinants of firm growth (Barney, 1991; Penrose, 1959) has not produced definitive results (Barba Navaretti et al., 2014; Brüderl & Preisendörfer, 2000; Cooper et al., 1994; Goedhuys et al., 2016; Goedhuys & Sleuwaegen, 2013; Levratto et al., 2010). The focus of the most recent research stream in this field has shifted to the impact of the environment as entrepreneurial ecosystems (EEs) on firm expansion. This monograph adopts a definition of the EE as interdependent actors and resources that generate productive entrepreneurship within a specific territory (Stam, 2018; Stam & Van De Ven, 2021). Thus, EE constitutes a concept of a system-oriented, functionally integrated environment of firms within a given geographic space (region, country).

In both research streams – the resource-based and the ecosystem-based – significant research gaps are observed regarding the conceptualization and measurement of growth and its determinants. First, by focusing on firm size expansion through the lens of revenues, these analyses overlook the expected outcomes in the form of economic efficiency, positive financial indicators, and social values. Meanwhile, growth is not an end in itself but a means to achieving economic outcomes, and it should be accompanied by the idea of productive entrepreneurship, which brings both economic and social value (Baumol, 1959). Second, research on the influence of EEs is still in an early stage of development, and no decisive conclusions about their impact have yet been reached (Stam, 2018; Stam & Van De Ven, 2021;

DOI: 10.4324/9781003739333-1

Xie et al., 2021). Third, the conceptualization of key concepts – namely, the essence and dimensions of ecosystems and productive entrepreneurship – is incomplete (Nicotra et al., 2018; Stam & Van De Ven, 2021).

The monograph conceptualizes productive entrepreneurship as sustainable high growth (SHG) of firms, i.e., growth that is continuing and generates both economic and social value. The proposed SHG concept integrates the ideas of productive entrepreneurship and high growth of firms, representing rapid growth that combines financial efficiency with social value in the form of increased employment.

Although their share in the business population is small, SHG firms constitute an important group due to their contribution to the economy. Their probability of coping with the intensive investments associated with scaling up and avoiding the risk of failure is higher than that of other firms. SHG firms also exhibit a higher likelihood of expanding into foreign markets and evolving into large enterprises. From the perspective of evolutionary economics, this particular group of firms forms a market niche, which, through the diffusion of development patterns imitated by other entities, may proliferate and influence the behavior of the broader population.

In response to the current state of knowledge and the identified research gaps, the research problem addressed in the dissertation concerns the impact of EEs on the SHG of firms. The main objective of the monograph is to develop conceptual foundations of the relationship between EEs and the firm's SHG and to empirically verify whether and how EEs impact SHG. The specific objectives include:

1 systematization of the concept of entrepreneurial ecosystems and research on their impact on productive entrepreneurship;
2 conceptualization of productive entrepreneurship as the SHG of firms;
3 development of measures of SHG and EEs;
4 identification of the relationships between the characteristics of EEs and the SHG of firms, including moderators of this relationship.

Based on the literature review, the following research hypotheses were formulated:

H1. Sustainable high growth of enterprises depends on the structural characteristics of entrepreneurial ecosystems.
H2. The heterogeneity of enterprises operating within entrepreneurial ecosystems moderates the impact of these ecosystems on the sustainable high growth of enterprises.
H2.1. The influence of entrepreneurial ecosystems on the sustainable high growth of enterprises is moderated by enterprise characteristics such as age, size, scope of operations, and knowledge intensity of their activities.

H2.2. Prior sustainable high growth of enterprises moderates the impact of entrepreneurial ecosystems on future sustainable high growth of these enterprises.

H3. The impact of entrepreneurial ecosystems on the sustainable high growth of enterprises is moderated by spatial interactions between proximate ecosystems.

The subject of the study is the relationship between the SHG of firms and the ecosystems of Polish voivodeships. The substantive, geographic, and temporal scope of the study encompasses the structural characteristics of firms and regions – understood as Polish voivodeships – in the years 2018–2022. The focus on administrative units is justified by both the availability of statistical data and the role of regional authorities in economic development policy. The involvement of regional governments in shaping EEs allows for practical implications and recommendations resulting from the study.

The research sample consisted of 43,714 firms, representative in terms of geographic distribution and industry structure. Unlike most studies relying on macrodata, this sample is based on firm-level microdata. The research methods included narrative and critical literature review (theoretical part) and secondary data analysis to verify the research hypotheses (empirical part). In conducting the secondary data analysis, econometric, statistical, and machine-learning techniques (spectral clustering) were applied. In addition, large-scale data processing techniques were used, including text mining, web scraping, and Geographic Information Systems and geostatistical methods.

The unique value of the findings rests in the explanation of how EEs can contribute to firms' SHG, using data from Polish regional ecosystems in the years 2018–2022. Our research provides theoretical, methodological, and practical contributions to the literature on EEs, to the research on entrepreneurial high growth, and to related policy areas.

First, regarding the research on EEs, this book proposes a theoretical advancement of the EE concept by conceptualizing the output of EEs as sustainable high-growth entrepreneurship. Moreover, this research acknowledges unique boundaries of ecosystems that do not necessarily follow the administrative units, such as regions, and thus contributes to the ongoing debate in this area.

Second, the monograph developed a method for measuring SHG and EEs, as well as the relationships between them, making a methodological contribution. Third, our findings bring a policy-relevant contribution. The identified EE characteristics and profiles conducive to SHG might serve as canvas for setting up entrepreneurship and regional policy directed at the upgrade of EEs (Brown & Mawson, 2019).

The monograph is structured into four chapters. Chapter 1 presents the nature of firm growth and discusses methods of its measurement. It provides a systematization of knowledge concerning the economic significance, essence, and determinants of high-growth enterprises. Chapter 2 will present the concept of the EE in conjunction with the SHG of firms. It will outline the structural characteristics and the differences in definitional approaches to EEs to come up with the hypotheses for empirical investigation. The chapter will conclude with an analysis of economic policy based on EEs. Chapter 3 outlines the methodology of the empirical study and presents the research framework. It specifies the methods and techniques used to verify the hypotheses, as well as a research sample. Chapter 4 will present the results of the empirical research. It was highlighted how the structural characteristics of EEs affect the SHG of firms. The findings also demonstrated how heterogeneity of enterprises and spatial interactions moderate the impact of EEs on the company's SHG. This is followed by a discussion of results, limitations, and recommendations for business and economic policy in an international context.

Bibliography

Barba Navaretti, G., Castellani, D., & Pieri, F. (2014). Age and firm growth: Evidence from three European countries. *Small Business Economics*, *43*(4), 823–837. https://doi.org/10.1007/s11187-014-9564-6

Barney, J. (1991). Firm resources and sustained competitive advantage. *Journal of Management*, *17*(1), 99–120.

Baumol, W. J. (1959). *Business behavior, value and growth*. Macmillan.

Birch, D. (1987). *Job Creation in America: How Our Smallest Companies Put the Most People to Work* (SSRN Scholarly Paper No. 1496185). https://papers.ssrn.com/abstract=1496185

Brnjas, Z., Vulićević, V., & Čanaićević, D. (2015). Importance and role of fast growing companies–Gazelles in modern economies. *Economic Analysis*, *48*(3–4), 44–61.

Brown, R., & Mawson, S. (2019). Entrepreneurial ecosystems and public policy in action: A critique of the latest industrial policy blockbuster. *Cambridge Journal of Regions, Economy and Society*, *12*(3), 347–368.

Brüderl, J., & Preisendörfer, P. (2000). Fast-growing businesses: Empirical evidence from a German study. *International Journal of Sociology*, *30*(3), 45–70. https://doi.org/10.1080/15579336.2000.11770218

Cooper, A. C., Gimeno-Gascon, F. J., & Woo, C. Y. (1994). Initial human and financial capital as predictors of new venture performance. *Journal of Business Venturing*, *9*(5), 371–395. https://doi.org/10.1016/0883-9026(94)90013-2

Davidsson, P. (2006). *Entrepreneurship and the growth of firms*. Edward Elgar Publishing Limited.

Gancarczyk, M. (2017). *The process of SME growth: Integrating the resource-based and transaction cost approaches*. Jagiellonian University Press.

Goedhuys, M., Mohnen, P., & Taha, T. (2016). Corruption, innovation and firm growth: Firm-level evidence from Egypt and Tunisia. *Eurasian Business Review*, *6*(3), 299–322. https://doi.org/10.1007/s40821-016-0062-4

Goedhuys, M., & Sleuwaegen, L. (2013). The impact of international standards certification on the performance of firms in less developed countries. *World Development, 47*, 87–101. https://doi.org/10.1016/j.worlddev.2013.02.014

Levratto, N., Zouikri, M., & Tessier, L. (2010). The determinants of growth for smes-a longitudinal study from french manufacturing firms. *Available at SSRN 1780466*. https://papers.ssrn.com/sol3/papers.cfm?abstract_id=1780466

Nicotra, M., Romano, M., Del Giudice, M., & Schillaci, C. E. (2018). The causal relation between entrepreneurial ecosystem and productive entrepreneurship: A measurement framework. *The Journal of Technology Transfer, 43*, 640–673.

Penrose, E. (1959). *Theory of the growth*. John Wiley & Sons.

Solmon, L. C. (2019). *Labor markets, employment policy, and job creation*. Routledge.

Stam, E. (2018). Measuring entrepreneurial ecosystems. In A. O'Connor, E. Stam, F. Sussan, & D. B. Audretsch (Eds.), *Entrepreneurial ecosystems* (Vol. 38, pp. 173–197). Springer International Publishing. https://doi.org/10.1007/978-3-319-63531-6_9

Stam, E., & Van De Ven, A. (2021). Entrepreneurial ecosystem elements. *Small Business Economics, 56*(2), 809–832. https://doi.org/10.1007/s11187-019-00270-6

Xie, Z., Wang, X., Xie, L., & Duan, K. (2021). Entrepreneurial ecosystem and the quality and quantity of regional entrepreneurship: A configurational approach. *Journal of Business Research, 128*, 499–509.

1 The essence and conditions for a high-growth enterprise

1.1 The essence and measurement of enterprise high growth

Growth represents an increase in the size of a company and is viewed in quantitative terms, most often through the dynamics of revenue, employment, asset value, market share, or level of diversification (Davidsson, 2006; Gancarczyk, 2017). Growth is usually accompanied by qualitative change in the form of the development of product or service innovation, business processes, or employee competencies. Development processes occur with varying intensity in every organization, and their nature is often evolutionary and incremental. Consequently, development without growth is also possible. Intensive growth, referred to as rapid or high growth, due to significant expansion of company size in a relatively short time, is a rare phenomenon observed in only small fractions of enterprises.

Growth may be organic or result from mergers with other companies (Henrekson & Johansson, 2010). Growth through mergers and acquisitions, by nature, does not introduce new value to the market but merely represents a rearrangement of resources among existing entities, most often motivated by cost considerations and the pursuit of market dominance. Organic growth, understood as the expansion of an organization based on implemented innovations and improvements, increases added value and value for society from the perspective of improving the utility of goods and services and quality of life (Davidsson, 2006; Gancarczyk, 2017). The strategy adopted by an enterprise not only influences growth but also moderates the relationship between growth and profitability. Research findings indicate that companies offering a wide range of products are better able to translate employment growth into financial performance (Senderovitz et al., 2016).

Continuous growth is one of the most important topics currently being studied. An inherent feature of growth is its lack of consistency over time (El-Dardiry & Vogt, 2023). Most enterprises experience growth only during certain periods (Daunfeldt & Halvarsson, 2015). The stability of growth rates depends on firm age – young companies exhibit greater variability in growth

DOI: 10.4324/9781003739333-2

rates. Growth stability increases when a firm possesses intangible assets such as patents, licenses, or utility models (Bianchini et al., 2017). Research shows that long-lasting periods of rapid growth are rather random in nature and do not result from structural characteristics of organizations (Moschella et al., 2019). Moreover, mathematical general equilibrium models point to irregular and short-lived episodes of rapid company growth (Carrillo-Tudela et al., 2021). High growth volatility may result in the crowding-out effect, where rapidly growing firms are replaced by others that achieve better performance at a given time, leading to permanent market dynamics (Falkenhall & Junkka, 2009). An interesting aspect of growth is its weak correlation with current economic conditions and market signals (Dosi et al., 2020).

Evolutionary theories assume a stable growth rate in consecutive periods. This is justified by the relative stability of firm characteristics, which do adapt to changes in the environment, but the changes are not breakthrough in nature. Moreover, competing firms, by imitating the products of pioneering innovators, limit their growth rate in the long term (Dosi et al., 2020). In contrast, stochastic approaches assume independence of growth rates over time and treat company growth as a random walk, which prevents planning of company resources and strategies as well as economic policy (Dosi et al., 2020). The lack of sufficiently long time series containing data on business growth makes it difficult to provide a definitive answer regarding the stability of growth rates (Dosi et al., 2020).

Another dilemma concerns the relationship between the growth rate of an industry and the growth of the enterprises operating within it. A study conducted by Dosi (2020) shows that there is a positive relationship between the growth rate of an industry and the variation in growth rates among the firms that comprise it (Dosi et al., 2020). Moreover, industries with a high dispersion of firm growth rates have a greater share of companies with long-term stable growth rates. The growth rate of an industry depends to a significant extent on its stage of development (Dosi et al., 2020; Geroski & Mazzucato, 2002).

However, a major research challenge is the heterogeneous nature of growth. Existing studies explain only a small portion of growth variance (around 15%), which greatly complicates growth forecasting (Coad, 2009; Goedhuys & Sleuwaegen, 2010). The difficulty of prediction is confirmed by investment firms seeking young companies with high growth potential. Their success rate in identifying gazelles is low: only 3 out of 20 invested firms turn out to be successful investments (Landström, 2007). The characteristics of firms vary in terms of their volatility. Some variables, such as the gender or education of the founder, remain constant for a given firm. Other variables, such as financial indicators, vary practically every year.

An additional challenge in research is posed by variables that are constant for firms within a particular industry or region (Chae, 2024). Growth determinants are highly heterogeneous geographically. Studies using quantile regression across 16 European countries revealed significant differences between nations (Hölzl, 2009). Even within individual countries, these factors are not homogeneous. For example, in Germany, population density positively influenced growth in the western regions, while in the eastern Länder, it had no statistically significant effect (Almus, 2002). More recent studies also demonstrate regional variation in the occurrence of gazelles, which is attributed to historical legacies (Tomenendal & Raffer, 2023).

The measurement of growth includes various indicators. The most commonly used are sales volume, profit, production volume, assets, and market share (Henrekson & Johansson, 2010; Khurana et al., 2008). Financial measures of growth efficiency are used less frequently, which makes it difficult to evaluate the outcomes of growth (Gancarczyk, 2017). The most important growth indicators are interrelated, and general relationships can be determined between them. It can be assumed that sales growth, with unchanged costs, will lead to increased employment, which serves to expand production and further sales. The growth of products and services sold enables the investment of cash surpluses into assets. Market share growth is less correlated with other indicators and depends largely on competitors' actions.

Each indicator has its limitations. Traditional asset value measurement can be problematic for companies with a significant share of intangible assets (Coad & Hölzl, 2012). Sales growth may be caused by cyclical fluctuations in sold products rather than innovations. Moreover, this indicator requires adjustment due to the decline in currency value over time, and in the case of studies conducted in countries using different currencies, an additional issue arises – currency conversion. Employment growth is important in economic policy and from the perspective of societal value, but it is less desirable from the entrepreneur's point of view (Gancarczyk, 2017).

In studies of growth dynamics, certain categories of firms are often excluded. One such limitation is the size of the enterprise at the beginning of the period. This is driven by the desire to remove the smallest entities from studies, in which, for example, the employment of a single worker would result in a 50 or 100% increase. The most common variables defining the threshold are sales revenue, employment, and age (Levratto et al., 2010).

The measurement methodology and the length of the period under consideration are further important aspects from the perspective of research results. Regarding the time range of growth measurement, most studies use a time horizon of three to five years (Audretsch et al., 2014), although longer periods have also been used, such as seven or even ten years (Bjuggren et al., 2013; Smallbone et al., 1995). Some researchers have also applied different thresholds for different firm size classes; for example, Storey used an annual 25% sales growth threshold for small firms and 15% for large firms (Storey, 2001).

Consistency of measurements over time enables comparison of results and trend analysis (Brnjas et al., 2015). The most commonly used methods include (Brnjas et al., 2015):

1 measurement of absolute values – the value of the analyzed indicator in the last period studied is reduced by the value in the first period;
2 measurement of relative values – the ratio of the indicator value in the last period to that in the first period is measured;
3 mixed method – a combination of the two above methods is used; the best known is the Birch index, measured as the product of absolute and relative growth, which is intended to reduce the tendency to identify high-growth firms mainly among large (absolute growth) or small (relative growth) enterprises.

The choice of growth indicator is extremely important for capturing its various aspects. For example, a company that outsources production will not show significant employment growth; therefore, sales growth is a better indicator for firms using this strategy (Shepherd & Wiklund, 2009). The purpose of the research also influences the choice of growth indicator. From the perspective of economic policy objectives, employment growth is often chosen due to its impact on reducing unemployment (Reyes, 2017). Survey studies show that sales growth is the preferred form of growth among entrepreneurs: 34% of companies declare this as a priority goal, 31% are interested in employment growth, 21% in increasing market share, and 16% in product and sales diversification (Medovnikov et al., 2023).

The OECD approach (OECD, 2009, 2010), which takes into account both employment size and revenue dynamics, is often used. It was developed further by Eurostat, which classified groups of enterprises based on growth. On this basis, the Polish Central Statistical Office (GUS), in its annual report "Entrepreneurship Indicators," identified the following categories of enterprises: high-growth enterprises (HGE) (average annual revenue growth of 20%), growth enterprises (10%), and stable enterprises (between −10% and 10%). The GUS study includes only enterprises employing more than nine persons that submitted the "Annual Enterprise Survey" (OECD, 2016, 2021).

1.2 Characteristics of high-growth enterprises and the conditions for high growth

Characteristics of high-growth enterprises

There is no consistency in the terminology used for the firms demonstrating high growth. The most commonly used terms today are *high-growth enterprises* and *gazelles*. The OECD (2009, 2010) defined HGE as one in which the average growth rate exceeds 20% over the past three years, the total growth over this period is at least 72.8%, and which employs a minimum of ten people. The OECD reserved the term *gazelles* for young firms less than five years old (Ahmad, 2006). Birch and Medoff (1994) defined gazelles as companies achieving at least 20% annual sales growth over a specified period, with a baseline year revenue of at least $100,000. Less conventional names for firms exhibiting rapid growth include superstar fast-growth firms (Coad & Rao, 2008) and rapidly expanding firms (Schreyer, 2000). There are also definitions in which gazelles are directly associated with firms experiencing periods of sudden growth (Kubičková et al., 2018). Their growth is difficult to predict, and thus, the appearance and disappearance of high-growth firms are largely stochastic (Bolek et al., 2021; Stam, 2010). In Australia, about half of high-growth firms record an uninterrupted four-year period of rapid growth, whereas the proportion of high-growth firms over a seven-year period falls to below 20% (Majeed et al., 2021). Another category of enterprises characterized by rapid growth is unicorns. This is a relatively small group of firms that have reached a valuation of 1 billion dollars within a short period (a few years). Since 2010, the number of unicorns has been steadily increasing, primarily financed by private funds.

In recent years, the concept of scale-up firms has emerged, which is similar to high-growth firms (Coad, 2024). In this concept, firm growth is based on scaling the business, that is, increasing the scale of operations (Jansen et al., 2023). Some authors distinguish gazelles from scale-up firms, noting that the latter are characterized by a higher growth rate (Jansen et al., 2023). In practice, scale-up firms are considered a subgroup of high-growth firms.

High-growth firms are characterized by above-average innovativeness. In Spain, high-growth firms allocate a proportionally larger share of their annual turnover to R&D expenses than growth firms, and the share of gazelles not engaging in such activities is about 25% of firms, roughly half the size of the corresponding share among growth firms. In Germany, the proportion of high-growth firms without an R&D department is nearly 9%, while more than 25% of firms employ at least one-quarter of their staff in research and development (Schreyer, 2000). Gazelles are often associated with high-tech sectors, but they can be found in virtually all sectors of the economy. Gazelles frequently produce technologically advanced products, which they sell to other firms, contributing to their technological growth.

Over the past 25 years, researchers have rarely examined how growth is related to financial performance (Davidsson et al., 2009). Gazelles demonstrating high profitability are more likely to achieve both high profitability and rapid growth than firms characterized solely by rapid growth. Furthermore, firm age is negatively associated with the financial productivity of growth (Mansikkamäki, 2023). Studies conducted in Poland found no relationship between board feminization and firm performance, whereas analyses from Slovenia indicate that the entrepreneur's gender affects the determinants of profitability in high-growth firms, providing further evidence of the extreme heterogeneity of these firms (Błach et al., 2025; Širec & Močnik, 2014).

We can distinguish three phases in the performance growth of HGEs. The first is the "valley of death," the period between a company's founding and obtaining external financing and stabilizing positive cash flows. Results during this period are most often negative. The next phase is a transitional period, during which the company records weak and highly variable results (Monteiro, 2019). The initial phases of a company's activity are characterized by chaotic resource allocation, which the firm tries to optimize as its operations evolve. The third phase is a sudden surge in performance, triggered by some activating force. This factor can be internal (e.g., increased innovativeness) or external (e.g., the emergence of a market opportunity) (Monteiro, 2019). Often, it is a combination of different events, where at least one factor is independent of the entrepreneur's actions.

HGEs are also highly adaptable and characterized by faster growth following a stagnation phase (Spitsin et al., 2023, 2024). Studies conducted in Slovenia (during the 2008 crisis) and selected European countries (COVID-19 crisis) also confirm the greater resilience of gazelles to crises (Bonča et al., 2018; Coad, Bauer et al., 2023). Crises impact economic centers and peripheries to varying degrees globally; such a dependency has not been demonstrated at the local level in studies of high-growth firms in the UK at the onset of the COVID-19 pandemic (Greene et al., 2020). In response to downturns, gazelles reduce investments disproportionately compared to other firms, and their sales also decline (Bonča et al., 2018; Coad, Amaral-Garcia et al., 2023). Employment (Bonča et al., 2018) and productivity (Coad, Amaral-Garcia et al., 2023) are the least sensitive to crises. During the pandemic, the vast majority of surveyed HGEs provided various types of emotional support to employees. Furthermore, work styles were adapted to remote work, reducing the risk of large outbreaks within firms and thus maintaining operational capacity (Greene et al., 2020).

Determinants of firm growth in empirical studies

Despite the passage of time, interest in studying the factors driving firm growth remains strong. Understanding these factors is highly significant from the perspective of business practice and economic policy. Since not all firms are capable of rapid growth, support measures must be targeted at firms that are either already experiencing fast growth or demonstrate the potential for it. The most fundamental classification of firm growth determinants distinguishes three main groups of factors: individual factors related to the entrepreneur, organizational factors concerning strategy and firm resources, and environmental factors (Zhou & De Wit, 2009). Sometimes, a fourth factor is added, intermediate between the environment and the firm, namely, the entrepreneur's network of contacts and collaboration with other entities (Reyes, 2017).

Factors related to the entrepreneur's characteristics

The first group of factors studied are the traits associated with the entrepreneur and the individuals managing the firm. These attributes were among the first determinants of growth to be investigated. The entrepreneur's level of education has played a key role in firm growth in numerous studies (Cooper et al., 1994; Devine et al., 2019; Teruel & De Wit, 2011), although not all studies have shown a clear relationship between the length of formal education and growth (Brüderl & Preisendörfer, 2000; Goedhuys & Sleuwaegen, 2010). Literature emphasizes that not only the education of the primary manager matters but also that of the entire top management team (Devine et al., 2019). Entrepreneurs with higher education tend to have greater ambitions, which does not directly translate into firm growth; however, a lack of ambition in an entrepreneur is a predictor of slower growth (Autio, 2009; Bosma et al., 2009). In addition, the costs associated with starting and running a firm, which prevent alternative employment in the open labor market, lead to higher expectations regarding performance and returns (Autio, 2009).

Psychological factors are also significant. In a study conducted by Teruel and De Wit (2011), three such factors were identified. Motivation in the form of income increase positively influenced firm growth. The anticipated proportion of individuals planning to start a business was associated with a higher share of high-growth firms in the economy. Likewise, the subjective perception of business growth opportunities positively correlates with the share of high-growth firms in the economy (Teruel & De Wit, 2011). Orser and Hogarth-Scott (2002) also observed a positive correlation between the growth-oriented decisions of opportunity-seeking individuals and the actual growth of the firm (Orser & Hogarth-Scott, 2002). Confidence can determine a firm's financial performance (Guluma, 2021). Entrepreneurs whose main motivation for starting a firm is the desire for independence are less inclined to pursue rapid firm growth (Glancey et al., 1998).

Research has also examined the influence of the entrepreneur's gender on firm growth. Some studies indicate that firms managed by men experienced faster growth (Cooper et al., 1994). This result can be explained by psychological differences between men and women. Men often pursue profit, whereas many women prioritize a balanced professional life and the pursuit of personal passions (Devine et al., 2019). However, not all studies confirm this relationship (Brüderl & Preisendörfer, 2000; Goedhuys & Sleuwaegen, 2010).

Studies have shown a negative relationship between the entrepreneur's age and firm growth (Stam & Wennberg, 2009). Similar findings indicate that high-growth firms managed by individuals under 45 exhibited faster growth, which may reflect older managers' poorer perception of market conditions and consequently less efficient exploitation of emerging opportunities (Barba Navaretti et al., 2014).

Previous professional experience has also been studied. Firms managed by individuals from entrepreneurial families did not show faster growth (Cooper et al., 1994). The entrepreneur's prior experience in a similar type of business was positively correlated with firm growth (Cooper et al., 1994; Devine et al., 2019), whereas the experience of other top management team members had no impact (Devine et al., 2019). Prior employment in non-profit organizations also had no statistical effect on firm growth (Cooper et al., 1994). Previous managerial experience, however, played a statistically significant role in shaping firm growth (Brüderl & Preisendörfer, 2000; Stam & Wennberg, 2009).

Firms that were founded as full-time endeavors experience faster growth (Brüderl & Preisendörfer, 2000). Individuals who leave their jobs to start a business often depend financially on its success and therefore strive for high financial performance. In contrast, those for whom it is an additional source of income are often satisfied with small but steady earnings. The owner's status was also studied, and it was found that state-managed firms exhibited lower growth (Moschella et al., 2019).

Factors related to the characteristics of the enterprise

The second key group of factors influencing growth are those related to the enterprise itself (Almus, 2002; Coad & Rao, 2008). Most studies note a decline in growth rates as the firm ages (Biggs & Srivastava, 1996). However, the relationship between firm age and growth is heterogeneous. Studies on African enterprises showed that firm age is statistically significantly negatively correlated with growth for the 70% of the oldest firms, while for the 30% youngest firms, the correlation is statistically insignificant (Goedhuys & Sleuwaegen, 2010). The heterogeneous nature of growth was also reported by Levratto (2010), who studied 12,811 firms over an 11-year period from 1997 to 2007. He distinguished three forms of growth: no growth (steady growth, growth close to zero), dynamic growth (1–20% annual growth), and rapid growth (over 20% annually). The negative effect of age was statistically significant in all the above groups of firms and increased with higher growth rates.

Another factor considered is collaboration between firms. Studies primarily focus on the impact of collaboration on enterprise innovation (Le Roy & Czakon, 2016). It has been established, for example, that companies operating within research networks with universities and research institutions are more likely to become high-growth firms (Caloghirou et al., 2022).

On the U.S. IT market, firms' financial results were significantly affected by the level of aggressive competitive actions compared to competitors' ventures. The same study showed that collaboration between firms played a key role in generating financial results in the IT sector (Young et al., 1996). Another seven-year study across 41 industries demonstrated that firms adopting less aggressive competition than their rivals may also experience a decline in market share (Ferrier et al., 1999). A high concentration of competitors in a firm's operating region positively affects growth. From these considerations, it can be concluded that a company's strategy, as determined by its management, plays a significant role in its financial performance.

Business networks are often regionally clustered, and geographic proximity facilitates benefits and thus enterprise growth. Establishing relationships among nearby firms promotes the diffusion of innovations, leading to faster growth, especially during the early stages of firm development (Funk, 2014). However, some studies indicate that geographic proximity can have a negative effect, while organizational and social similarities have a positive influence (Shkolnykova, 2023). Other studies indicate that geographical proximity and other types of proximity are positively correlated, so in studies that consider both types within a given category, geographical proximity loses. Attention is also drawn to the difficulties in coordinating cooperation between firms located far apart (Alnuaimi et al., 2012).

Firms that act as network hubs gain faster access to innovation and have a stronger social position among enterprises, which can be translated into performance (Gnyawali & Madhavan, 2001). Furthermore, firms displaying an aggressive position and a high level of coopetition with other firms achieve better financial results.

Firms established as spin-offs experience faster growth, which is most likely due to financial support and non-material assistance. Thanks to financial injections and organizational support, spin-offs build their resource base faster and can benefit from the experience of the parent company, using its network of contacts and sales markets (Hayter, 2013; Mohr et al., 2014).

The involvement of owners in management structures had a positive impact on growth (Arrighetti & Lasagni, 2013). Moreover, the probability of achieving rapid growth is higher for small and young firms. The negative effect of family ownership diminishes with the age of the firm (Bjuggren et al., 2013). A larger number of individuals in managerial roles positively influenced firm growth (Cooper et al., 1994; Devine et al., 2019).

High-tech firms that did not sell their shares to investors experienced faster growth (Mohr et al., 2014). The sale of shares or stock increases the number of individuals controlling the firm, thereby reducing decision-making power. The expansion of decision-making structures results in slower decision-making processes and diluted responsibility (Mohr et al., 2014). Innovation-based strategies are typical of gazelles and have a positive impact on firm growth (Brüderl & Preisendörfer, 2000; Sheppard, 2010).

Enterprises with dominant foreign capital are more likely to achieve gazelle status. Firms with a foreign owner had a 3.5% higher probability of becoming a gazelle (Cuaresma et al., 2014). The owner's origin from a specific part of the world did not affect growth (Goedhuys & Sleuwaegen, 2010). High start-up capital and employment also positively influence firm performance (Brüderl & Preisendörfer, 2000).

The results of analyses on the impact of innovation capabilities on firm growth are inconclusive. This is largely due to delays in implementing innovations within firms, which in turn do not immediately affect company performance (Biggs & Srivastava, 1996). R&D activity generally has a positive impact on firm growth (Goedhuys & Sleuwaegen, 2016).

The share of sales from new or significantly improved products influences growth, whereas process innovations do not show such an effect (Goedhuys & Sleuwaegen, 2010). Babina and her team discovered that firms investing in AI technologies experience faster growth in sales, employment, and market share. The authors assume that increased product innovation is the cause of this effect (Babina et al., 2024). Research conducted in Slovakia shows that the most important outcomes of introducing innovations are increased sales and attracting new customers. Equally important are increased customer satisfaction and brand recognition, which may indirectly contribute to growth (Benešová et al., 2018). Entrepreneurs themselves also point to the crucial role of innovation in business success; however, not all studies confirmed the impact of innovation investment and implemented product innovations on firm growth (Moschella et al., 2019). Likewise, the number of patents held by a company did not matter (Devine et al., 2019; Mohr et al., 2014). On the other hand, investment by enterprises in environmental innovations positively affected their growth (Colombelli et al., 2021).

Firms possessing a large amount of intangible assets have, on average, a higher chance of becoming high-growth firms (Bianchini et al., 2017). However, the effect is uneven. It is mainly observed in firms older than five years. In younger firms, a large share of intangible assets in total assets has a negative impact. This may suggest that acquiring intangible assets, especially those resulting from R&D activities, and increasing brand and trademark value require time. For firms older than five years, the effect is stronger for service companies than manufacturing firms (Du & Temouri, 2015). In developing countries, it is important to study aspects that are considered standard in highly developed economies. One example is having a website. It was irrelevant in Central Africa (Goedhuys & Sleuwaegen, 2010), but had an impact on growth in North African countries (Goedhuys et al., 2016).

Higher education among employees had an impact on growth (Goedhuys et al., 2016), as did the share of employees holding a master's or doctoral degree (Caloghirou et al., 2022). Not only the level of education matters but also the specific specialization. Technical higher education among employees had a greater impact on growth than university education in other disciplines (Herstad et al., 2013). Despite the influence of higher education level on growth, not all educational experiences matter. Employee training programs had no such effect (Caloghirou et al., 2022; Goedhuys & Sleuwaegen, 2010).

The studies also confirm the link between human capital and growth. Research has shown that the average level of wages was significant for firm growth (Du & Temouri, 2015). Labor costs measured as salaries and other related costs had either a positive (Barba Navaretti et al., 2014) or negative (Levratto et al., 2010) effect on growth depending on the study. Paying bonuses increased a firm's chances of becoming a gazelle by 8.5% (Rasmussen et al., 2018). This may be explained by the motivational role of bonuses, which encourage employees to work harder. Lopez-Garcia and Puente (2012) included wage premium as a dependent variable, defined as the average salary in a company compared to the average salary in other companies in the sector. A positive wage premium turned out to be statistically positively correlated with firm growth.

Financial indicators are among the most important predictors of the growth rate of enterprises, especially when combined with other types of variables (Srhoj, 2022; Weinblat, 2018). Research has shown that the level of debt matters for growth (Fernández-López et al., 2019), but the structure of financing is also important. The ratio of total financial debt and trade debt to total liabilities was significant for firm growth (Levratto et al., 2010). On the other hand, the combined share of long-term and total short- and long-term debt had no effect on growth rates (Lopez-Garcia & Puente, 2012). According to some studies, the leverage ratio had no impact on growth (Grinberger & Nehrebecka, 2015; Moschella et al., 2019), though not all research confirms this relationship (Bianchini et al., 2017). The EBITDA-to-sales ratio was also significant for the growth rate (Barba Navaretti et al., 2014). Profit from the previous year did not affect growth (Levratto et al., 2010). Another indicator that influenced firm growth was a high cash liquidity ratio (Grinberger & Nehrebecka, 2015). The quick ratio (current ratio II) was also positively correlated with growth. High cash flows, however, had a negative effect on growth rate. Return on assets (ROA) had no impact on firm growth (Bianchini et al., 2017; Fernández-López et al., 2019). No relationship was found in the case of return on equity (ROE) (Arrighetti & Lasagni, 2013; Grinberger & Nehrebecka, 2015). Return on investment (ROI) was also not significant for firm growth (Grinberger & Nehrebecka, 2015). Disclosure of financial information by a company is positively correlated with its growth, which may be explained by reduced information asymmetry and better allocation of financial resources from external investors (Khurana et al., 2008).

The source of financing is considered one of the growth factors. Receiving financial help had a negative effect in a study of 798 Polish companies in the years 1998–2012 (Grinberger & Nehrebecka, 2015). In studies conducted in Nigeria, winners of business plan competitions employed more people, generated higher profits, and had higher chances of survival (McKenzie, 2017). This can be interpreted in two ways. On the one hand, better-capitalized entrepreneurs have a better start and higher chances of surviving difficult times. On the other hand, funding was awarded to authors of the best ideas, which suggests the strong importance of the human factor.

Environmental factors

Environmental factors depend on the scale at which they are examined. We can distinguish a global scale, a macroscale (national level), a mesoscale (regions/voivodeships), and a microscale (counties, cities). Each level of the environment influences both the level above and the one below it. Thus, changes in the microenvironment contribute to changes in the economy of the entire country, and even globally.

In previous research, environmental factors have been examined mainly at the national level (Bianchini et al., 2017; Pereira & Temouri, 2018), and studies at smaller scales have been few (Stam & Van De Ven, 2021). Studied the growth of small firms from a local perspective, with particular emphasis on performance. The authors observed that small enterprises display faster growth in peripheral areas.

Other studies indicate that business growth in less developed regions is largely based on lower labor and resource costs. Although high-growth firms can be found in various geographical regions, locations rich in infrastructure stimulate rapid growth (Goswami et al., 2019). Likewise, high population density, which ensures easy access to capital, has a positive effect on growth (Sleuwaegen & Ramboer, 2020). The location of a business in a capital region should have a positive impact on enterprise growth due to easy access to skilled labor, markets, and developed technical infrastructure. This relationship has also been demonstrated in empirical studies (Giner et al., 2017; Levratto et al., 2010).

The location of a firm in highly developed countries, where a high GDP is an indicator of development, had a positive influence on business growth measured by sales volume, asset size, and employment (Anton, 2019). The absolute measure of economic size proved to be a more accurate predictor than economic growth itself. GDP growth had a positive effect only on growth measured by sales and assets, but not on growth measured by employment (Anton, 2019). Productivity measured as value per employee was relevant to growth (Bianchini et al., 2017; Levratto et al., 2010). Cuaresma showed that a 10% increase in total factor prodictivity (TFP) in a firm increases the likelihood of achieving gazelle status by 1–2%; however, firm age and size were better predictors (Cuaresma et al., 2014). Not all studies, however, confirm the impact of TFP on growth (Arrighetti & Lasagni, 2013).

Macroeconomic and financial environment factors have been considered as influencing growth. The level of development of the financial sector, measured by the size of bank deposits relative to GDP, had a negative impact on growth measured by employment size (Anton, 2019). Easy access to credit, proxied by a high ratio of credit to GDP, positively affects the growth of high-growth firms in European Union economies. Bank market concentration, however, had no significant effect on growth (Anton, 2019).

The production size of a sector was another factor that could be linked to high growth rates. A higher likelihood of high growth is observed in sectors with high production levels, which serve as a proxy for overall demand for products in a given industry (Arrighetti & Lasagni, 2013). However, sector growth is not a universal factor directly determining firm growth: in Austria, the opposite relationship was observed (Hölzl, 2014).

A high level of education in society improves firm performance, which can be explained in three ways. First, highly educated employees positively influence productivity. Second, a high proportion of university graduates in the population usually indicates a large number of universities, which positively affects knowledge spillovers and their transfer to firms. Third, it may cause a shift in demand toward more advanced products, which can increase firm competitiveness. Studies conducted in 17 European countries found a relationship between the proportion of students aged 18–23 and the share of high-growth firms in the country's economy (Teruel & De Wit, 2011).

Institutional factors also affect firm growth. Growth is constrained in countries with strong employee protection (Cuaresma et al., 2014; Teruel & De Wit, 2011). The authors point to two mechanisms: first, strong employee protection reduces incentives to start a firm due to a "safe haven" effect, as permanent employment is relatively more attractive. Second, firms grow faster when they are not constrained by fears of hiring employees and can replace underperforming staff (Teruel & De Wit, 2011). Another institutional factor influencing growth is the ease of starting a business, measured by the number of procedures required. Lower administrative burden increases the share of high-growth firms in the economy (Teruel & De Wit, 2011).

The stability of administrative procedures also positively impacts firm growth. Well-established procedures are resilient to political changes in the country (Pereira & Temouri, 2018). In Central and Eastern Europe, an increase of 1 point on a 0–4 scale measuring the state's friendliness toward entrepreneurs increases the probability of achieving high growth by 2.4% (Cuaresma et al., 2014). However, in countries perceived as corrupt or with high crime rates, a larger number of high-growth firms is observed. This may result from the perception of these factors by less successful firms, interpreting them as enabling conditions for fast-growing firms that exploit market imperfections unfairly (Cuaresma et al., 2014).

Other institutional barriers that hinder the development of high-growth firms include limited access to capital and a complex tax system with high taxes (Cuaresma et al., 2014). Furthermore, corruption affects firm growth since it undermines trust in the market and diverts investment, leaving high-potential growth firms underfunded (Goedhuys et al., 2016). A positive influence on firm growth is also exerted by the investment climate. Pereira and Temouri classify as such all investment risks not considered political, economic, or financial. In particular, a low risk of expropriation of firm assets and prompt payment terms by clients are positive factors (Pereira & Temouri, 2018).

Despite several decades of intensive study, conclusive results regarding the impact of the entrepreneur-, firm-, strategy-, and environment-related factors on firm growth have not yet been obtained. Considering these research areas, the studied antecedents of high growth focused predominantly on the resource-based factors, while the external environment remained less explored. Consequently, in recent years, attention has shifted toward a systemic approach to environmental factors, reflected in the concept of entrepreneurial ecosystems (EE), which will be presented in Chapter 2.

1.3 The role of high-growth enterprises in the economy

In the early 1980s, D. Birch (1981) observed a disproportionately large impact of HGE on employment. Two-thirds of new jobs created between 1969 and 1982 were generated by firms employing fewer than 21 people, and 82% by firms with fewer than 100 employees. Birch also noted that as much as 80% of new positions were created by firms no older than four years. Thus, he challenged the prevailing view that large companies were primarily responsible for creating new jobs. In subsequent years, he continued to study the relationship between company size and the jobs they create. Over ten years later, Birch concluded that it is not the size of a firm that determines its contribution to job creation. The driving force in the labor market is a category of firms that Birch called *gazelles*. By this term, he meant companies characterized by high growth rates and innovativeness, which add value to the economy. Only 4% of companies in the USA create 70% of new jobs (Brnjas et al., 2015; Solmon, 2019).

However, Birch's findings raise questions regarding their universality across time, space, and sectors (Schreyer, 2000). High-growth firms significantly strengthen local economies by generating new jobs rather than merely replacing old ones (Schreyer, 2000). They are seen as engines of development and centers from which innovation diffuses (Hölzl, 2014). For this reason, high-growth firms are an important subject of study from the perspective of economic policy (Acs et al., 2015; Brnjas et al., 2015). Nevertheless, the contribution of high-growth firms to the economy is not stable over time and is subject to significant fluctuations, which complicates the study of their impact (Shepherd & Wiklund, 2009).

Another study was conducted using data from France, Italy, the Netherlands, Sweden, and the province of Quebec in Canada (Schreyer, 2000). The author examined the impact of high-growth firms on job creation. For this purpose, the top 10% of the fastest-growing firms among growing firms were selected. The share of high-growth firms in these countries ranges from 2 to 5%, and the share of new jobs varies by country, from around 30 to over 60%. Within high-growth firms, the largest companies, with more than 500 employees, contributed most to the creation of new jobs, and with each smaller size class, the average annual employment growth decreases. In each analyzed country, the share of small and medium-sized firms in creating new jobs was lower among growth firms than among high-growth firms (Schreyer, 2000).

While the relationship between high-growth firms and job creation has been relatively well studied, the connection between productivity and high-growth firms is relatively underexplored (Du & Temouri, 2015). Total factor productivity is considered one of the most important factors influencing long-term growth and its short-term fluctuations. Higher productivity and access to new resources and markets imply growth, which in turn generates feedback in the form of increased productivity. There are several reasons to believe in a link between productivity and high-growth firms. High-growth firms are able to convert previous investments into innovations. Studies show that innovativeness is a characteristic that can be attributed to most gazelles, and the growth rate of these firms can be up to twice as high as that of non-innovative firms (Brown et al., 2012; Mason & Brown, 2010). Innovations are seen as a key driver of productivity growth in the United States, whereas the weaker growth performance of European firms may be associated with lower levels of innovation on the continent (Oliner et al., 2008). High-growth firms are creators of technological knowledge, and the faster their growth, the greater their contribution (Colombelli et al., 2014).

The literature also emphasizes the influence of productivity on the geographic scope of a firm's operations. High-growth firms are often strongly connected to international markets. They are not limited to their own region or country but are oriented toward international activities. This phenomenon is attributed to their awareness of superior productivity compared to the average foreign firm, motivating them to expand. A firm with higher productivity should have a competitive advantage over less productive rivals (Du & Temouri, 2015; Greenaway & Kneller, 2007). High internationalization ensures that HGEs have a global economic impact. Entering a foreign market is often associated with increased productivity, especially for firms that previously had little exposure to international markets (Greenaway & Kneller, 2007). For this reason, productivity can be considered both a driving force behind the growth of HGEs and a consequence of that growth (Du & Temouri, 2015). Attention is also drawn to the flip side: productivity growth may lead to an increase in unemployment.

HGEs account for 30% of aggregated economic growth (Sedlacek & Ignaszak, 2021). A positive correlation has also been observed between GDP growth and the share of gazelles in a country's economy (Wajsman et al., 2019). Recently, attention has been drawn to the declining role of gazelles in the US economy (Sterk et al., 2021). The share of high-growth firms in the total number of enterprises, overall employment, and average firm size three to five years after their establishment are used as indicators of a firm's performance (OECD, 2016).

The social role of high-growth firms is relatively rarely mentioned – they can inspire other business owners and individuals aspiring to start a company (Teruel & De Wit, 2011). Many entrepreneurs, when founding or managing their firm, take high-growth firms as role models. Some of these enterprises are established as social enterprises with the mission of enhancing societal welfare (Cattafi et al., 2023).

Due to their economic significance, HGEs should be supported with public funds, but such support should be distinguished from SME support programs that exist in many countries. Public assistance programs for small and medium-sized enterprises are often based on size classes. Tying public support to employment size may discourage firms from increasing employment, thereby reducing the efficiency of these firms and the overall economy. Support programs for HGEs, however, are controversial. Some argue that these firms perform well on their own and do not need support, especially since public assistance should target entities affected by market failures, which HGEs typically are not (Hölzl, 2014). More often, the view is expressed that gazelles should be supported due to their significant impact on the economy, which contributes to more effective use of funds than if resources were directed to newly established firms or companies struggling to survive in the market (OECD, 2009, 2010).

Bibliography

Acs, Z. J. (2008). Foundations of high impact entrepreneurship. *Foundations and Trends® in Entrepreneurship*, *4*(6), 535–620.

Acs, Z. J. (Ed. Acs, Z. J.) (2010). High-impact entrepreneurship. In *Handbook of entrepreneurship research: An interdisciplinary survey and introduction*. Springer US. https://doi.org/10.1007/b105789

Acs, Z. J. (Ed. Acs, Z. J.) (2015). High-impact firms: Gazelles revisited. In *Global entrepreneurship, institutions and incentives* (pp. 542–583). Edward Elgar Publishing. https://www.elgaronline.com/downloadpdf/monochap/9781784718046.00041.pdf

Acs, Z. J., Autio, E., & Szerb, L. (Ed. Acs, Z. J.) (2015). National systems of entrepreneurship: Measurement issues and policy implications. In *Global entrepreneurship, institutions and incentives* (pp. 523–541). Edward Elgar Publishing. https://www.elgaronline.com/downloadpdf/monochap/9781784718046.00040.pdf

Ahmad, N. (2006). *A proposed framework for business demography statistics* (OECD Statistics Working Paper No. 2006/3). OECD Publishing. https://econpapers.repec.org/paper/oecstdaaa/2006_2f3-en.htm

Almus, M. (2002). What characterizes a fast-growing firm? *Applied Economics*, *34*(12), 1497–1508. https://doi.org/10.1080/00036840110105010

Alnuaimi, T., Opsahl, T., & George, G. (2012). Innovating in the periphery: The impact of local and foreign inventor mobility on the value of Indian patents. *Research Policy*, *41*(9), 1534–1543.

Anton, S. G. (2019). Leverage and firm growth: An empirical investigation of gazelles from emerging Europe. *International Entrepreneurship and Management Journal*, *15*(1), 209–232. https://doi.org/10.1007/s11365-018-0524-5

Arrighetti, A., & Lasagni, A. (2013). Assessing the determinants of high-growth manufacturing firms in Italy. *International Journal of the Economics of Business*, *20*(2), 245–267. https://doi.org/10.1080/13571516.2013.783456

Audretsch, D. B., Coad, A., & Segarra, A. (2014). Firm growth and innovation. *Small Business Economics*, *43*(4), 743–749. https://doi.org/10.1007/s11187-014-9560-x

Autio, E. (2009). *The Finnish paradox: The curious absence of high-growth entrepreneurship in Finland*. ETLA Discussion Papers. https://www.econstor.eu/handle/10419/44561

Babina, T., Fedyk, A., He, A., & Hodson, J. (2024). Artificial intelligence, firm growth, and product innovation. *Journal of Financial Economics*, *151*, 103745. https://doi.org/10.1016/j.jfineco.2023.103745

Barba Navaretti, G., Castellani, D., & Pieri, F. (2014). Age and firm growth: Evidence from three European countries. *Small Business Economics*, *43*(4), 823–837. https://doi.org/10.1007/s11187-014-9564-6

Benešová, D., Kubičková, V., Michálková, A., & Krošláková, M. (2018). Innovation activities of gazelles in business services as a factor of sustainable growth in the Slovak Republic. *Entrepreneurship and Sustainability Issues*, *5*(3), 452–466.

Bianchini, S., Bottazzi, G., & Tamagni, F. (2017). What does (not) characterize persistent corporate high-growth? *Small Business Economics*, *48*(3), 633–656. https://doi.org/10.1007/s11187-016-9790-1

Biggs, T., & Srivastava, P. (1996). *Structural aspects of manufacturing in sub-Saharan Africa: Findings from a seven country enterprise survey* (Vol. 346). World Bank Publications. https://books.google.com/books?hl=en&lr=&id=qQdFMK5gB9IC&oi=fnd&pg=PR7&dq=Biggs+and+Srivastava+(1996&ots=vrePdfZqo0&sig=Fpk2cheHWb9XHwaWQYmfOu93XlI

Birch, D. L. (1981). Who creates jobs? *The Public Interest*, *65*, 3.

Birch, D., & Medoff, J. (Ed. Birch, D.) (1994). Gazelles. In *Labor markets, employment policy, and job creation*. Avalon Publishing, 1–429.

Bjuggren, C. M., Daunfeldt, S.-O., & Johansson, D. (2013). High-growth firms and family ownership. *Journal of Small Business and Entrepreneurship*, *26*(4), 365–385. https://doi.org/10.1080/08276331.2013.821765

Błach, J., Bukalska, E., Kaźmierska-Jóźwiak, B., & Pesa, A. R. (2025). Sustainability performance, corporate governance, and financial performance: Evidence from Poland and Central European listed companies. *Journal of Entrepreneurship*, *21*(1), 58–80.

Bolek, M., Pietraszewski, P., & Wolski, R. (2021). Companies' growth vs. growth opportunity: Evidence from the regular and alternative stock markets in Poland. *Acta Oeconomica*, *71*(2), 279–307.

Bonča, P. D., Tajnikar, M., Ponikvar, N., & Mörec, B. (2018). Firm growth types and key macroeconomic aggregates through the economic cycle. *Journal of Business Economics and Management*, *19*(1), 138–153.

Bosma, N., & Schutjens, V. (2009). Determinants of early-stage entrepreneurial activity in European regions: distinguishing low and high ambition entrepreneurship. In *Entrepreneurship and growth in local, regional and national economies*. Edward Elgar Publishing, 49–80.

Brnjas, Z., Vulićević, V., & Čanaićević, D. (2015). Importance and role of fast growing companies–Gazelles in modern economies. *Economic Analysis*, *48*(3–4), 44–61.

Brown, R., Hart, M., Mason, C., & Richmond, K. (2012). The growth dynamics of technology-based firms in Scotland. *Fraser of Allander Economic Commentary*, *36*(1), 56–65.

Brüderl, J., & Preisendörfer, P. (2000). Fast-growing businesses: Empirical evidence from a German study. *International Journal of Sociology*, *30*(3), 45–70. https://doi.org/10.1080/15579336.2000.11770218

Caloghirou, Y., Giotopoulos, I., Kontolaimou, A., & Tsakanikas, A. (2022). Inside the black box of high-growth firms in a crisis-hit economy: Corporate strategy, employee human capital and R&D capabilities. *International Entrepreneurship and Management Journal*, *18*(3), 1319–1345. https://doi.org/10.1007/s11365-020-00674-x

Carrillo-Tudela, C., Clymo, A., & Coles, M. G. (2021). *Equilibrium Job Turnover and the Business Cycle*. https://papers.ssrn.com/sol3/papers.cfm?abstract_id=4026574

Cattafi, G., Del Pozzo, A., & Nicolò, D. (2023). People first! Intellectual capital and growth of high-growth social cooperatives (social gazelles) in the startup stage. Evidence from Italy. *Piccola Impresa/Small Business*, *1*. https://journals.uniurb.it/index.php/piccola/article/view/3500

Chae, H.-C. (2024). In search of gazelles: Machine learning prediction for Korean high-growth firms. *Small Business Economics*, *62*(1), 243–284. https://doi.org/10.1007/s11187-023-00760-8

Coad, A. (Ed. Coad, A.) (2009). The growth of firms: A survey of theories and empirical evidence. In *The growth of firms: A survey of theories and empirical evidence*. Edward Elgar Publishing Ltd, 1–208.

Coad, A. (2024). *Scale-ups and high-growth firms: Theory, definitions, and measurement*. Springer Nature.

Coad, A., Amaral-Garcia, S., Bauer, P., Domnick, C., Harasztosi, P., Pál, R., & Teruel, M. (2023). Investment expectations by vulnerable European firms in times of COVID. *Eurasian Business Review*, *13*(1), 193–220. https://doi.org/10.1007/s40821-022-00218-z

Coad, A., Bauer, P., Domnick, C., Harasztosi, P., Pál, R., & Teruel, M. (2023). From rapid decline to high growth: Where in the distribution did COVID hit hardest? *Journal of Small Business and Enterprise Development*, *30*(6), 1178–1209.

Coad, A., & Hölzl, W. (Ed. Coad, A.) (2012). Firm growth: Empirical analysis. In *Handbook on the economics and theory of the firm*. Edward Elgar Publishing, 324–339.

Coad, A., & Rao, R. (2008). Innovation and firm growth in high-tech sectors: A quantile regression approach. *Research Policy*, *37*(4), 633–648. Scopus. https://doi.org/10.1016/j.respol.2008.01.003

Colombelli, A., Krafft, J., & Quatraro, F. (2014). High-growth firms and technological knowledge: Do gazelles follow exploration or exploitation strategies? *Industrial and Corporate Change*, *23*(1), 261–291.

Colombelli, A., Krafft, J., & Quatraro, F. (2021). Firms' growth, green gazelles and eco-innovation: Evidence from a sample of European firms. *Small Business Economics*, *56*(4), 1721–1738. https://doi.org/10.1007/s11187-019-00236-8

Cooper, A. C., Gimeno-Gascon, F. J., & Woo, C. Y. (1994). Initial human and financial capital as predictors of new venture performance. *Journal of Business Venturing*, *9*(5), 371–395. https://doi.org/10.1016/0883-9026(94)90013-2

Cuaresma, J. C., Oberhofer, H., & Vincelette, G. A. (2014). Firm growth and productivity in Belarus: New empirical evidence from the machine building industry. *Journal of Comparative Economics*, *42*(3), 726–738.

Daunfeldt, S.-O., & Halvarsson, D. (2015). Are high-growth firms one-hit wonders? Evidence from Sweden. *Small Business Economics*, *44*, 361–383.

Davidsson, P. (2006). *Entrepreneurship and the growth of firms*. Edward Elgar Publishing Limited.

Davidsson, P., Steffens, P., & Fitzsimmons, J. (2009). Growing profitable or growing from profits: Putting the horse in front of the cart? *Journal of Business Venturing, 24*(4), 388–406. https://doi.org/10.1016/j.jbusvent.2008.04.003

Devine, R. A., Molina-Sieiro, G., Holmes, R. M., & Terjesen, S. A. (2019). Female-led high-growth: Examining the role of human and financial resource management: Journal of small business management. *Journal of Small Business Management, 57*(1), 81–109. https://doi.org/10.1111/jsbm.12492

Dosi, G., Grazzi, M., Moschella, D., Pisano, G., & Tamagni, F. (2020). Long-term firm growth: An empirical analysis of US manufacturers 1959–2015. *Industrial and Corporate Change, 29*(2), 309–332. https://doi.org/10.1093/icc/dtz044

Du, J., & Temouri, Y. (2015). High-growth firms and productivity: Evidence from the United Kingdom. *Small Business Economics, 44*(1), 123–143. https://doi.org/10.1007/s11187-014-9584-2

El-Dardiry, R., & Vogt, B. (2023). How far do Gazelles run? - Growth patterns of regular firms, high growth firms and startups. *Applied Economics, 55*(37), 4304–4318. https://doi.org/10.1080/00036846.2022.2128184

Falkenhall, B., & Junkka, F. (2009). High-growth firms in Sweden 1997–2007. *Characteristics and Development Patterns. The Swedish Agency for Growth Policy Analysis, Stockholm.* https://www.tillvaxtanalys.se/download/18.62dd45451715a00666f1c53b/1586366167362/WP_2009_05_en.pdf

Fernández-López, S., Rodeiro-Pazos, D., García González, F., & Rodríguez-Gulías, M. J. (2019). Determinants of high-growth university spin-offs in Spain. *Journal of Science and Technology Policy Management, 10*(4), 890–904.

Ferrier, W. J., Smith, K. G., & Grimm, C. M. (1999). The role of competitive action in market share erosion and industry dethronement: A study of industry leaders and challengers. *Academy of Management Journal, 42*(4), 372–388. https://doi.org/10.2307/257009

Funk, R. J. (2014). Making the most of where you are: Geography, networks, and innovation in organizations. *Academy of Management Journal, 57*(1), 193–222. https://doi.org/10.5465/amj.2012.0585

Gancarczyk, M. (2017). *The process of SME growth: Integrating the resource-based and transaction cost approaches*. Jagiellonian University Press.

Geroski, P., & Mazzucato, M. (2002). Learning and the sources of corporate growth. *Industrial and Corporate Change, 11*(4), 623–644.

Giner, J. M., Santa-María, M. J., & Fuster, A. (2017). High-growth firms: Does location matter? *International Entrepreneurship and Management Journal, 13*(1), 75–96. https://doi.org/10.1007/s11365-016-0392-9

Glancey, K., Greig, M., & Pettigrew, M. (1998). Entrepreneurial dynamics in small business service firms. *International Journal of Entrepreneurial Behavior & Research, 4*(3), 249–268.

Gnyawali, D. R., & Madhavan, R. (2001). Cooperative networks and competitive dynamics: A structural embeddedness perspective. *The Academy of Management Review, 26*(3), 431. https://doi.org/10.2307/259186

Goedhuys, M., Mohnen, P., & Taha, T. (2016). Corruption, innovation and firm growth: Firm-level evidence from Egypt and Tunisia. *Eurasian Business Review, 6*(3), 299–322. https://doi.org/10.1007/s40821-016-0062-4

Goedhuys, M., & Sleuwaegen, L. (2010). High-growth entrepreneurial firms in Africa: A quantile regression approach. *Small Business Economics, 34*(1), 31–51. https://doi.org/10.1007/s11187-009-9193-7

Goedhuys, M., & Sleuwaegen, L. (2016). High-growth versus declining firms: The differential impact of human capital and R&D. *Applied Economics Letters, 23*(5), 369–372. https://doi.org/10.1080/13504851.2015.1076139

Goswami, A. G., Medvedev, D., & Olafsen, E. (2019). *High-growth firms: Facts, fiction, and policy options for emerging economies*. World Bank Publications. https://books.google.com/books?hl=en&lr=&id=6NKIDwAAQBAJ&oi=fnd&pg=PT10&dq=Goswami,+Medvedev+%26+Olafsen,+2019&ots=S4HX2y5jZz&sig=6tfW_OBymCfJcMKtTqAmM2h5jac

Greenaway, D., & Kneller, R. (2007). Firm heterogeneity, exporting and foreign direct investment. *The Economic Journal, 117*(517), F134–F161.

Greene, F. J., Rosiello, A., Golra, O., & Vidmar, M. (2020). Analysing resilience in high growth firms at the onset of COVID-19 crisis. *Productivity Insights Nework*. https://www.researchgate.net/profile/Owais-Golra/publication/348000108_Analysing_Resilience_in_High_Growth_Firms_at_the_Onset_of_COVID-19_Crisis/links/5fec630545851553a0056bf4/Analysing-Resilience-in-High-Growth-Firms-at-the-Onset-of-COVID-19-Crisis.pdf

Grinberger, P., & Nehrebecka, N. (2015). Determinanty wzrostu polskich przedsiębiorstw giełdowych. *Ekonomia. Rynek, Gospodarka, Społeczeństwo, 43*, 41–65.

Guluma, T. F. (2021). The impact of corporate governance measures on firm performance: The influences of managerial overconfidence. *Future Business Journal, 7*(1), 50. https://doi.org/10.1186/s43093-021-00093-6

Hayter, C. S. (2013). Harnessing university entrepreneurship for economic growth: Factors of success among university spin-offs. *Economic Development Quarterly, 27*(1), 18–28. https://doi.org/10.1177/0891242412471845

Henrekson, M., & Johansson, D. (2010). Gazelles as job creators: A survey and interpretation of the evidence. *Small Business Economics, 35*(2), 227–244. https://doi.org/10.1007/s11187-009-9172-z

Herstad, S. J., Sandven, T., & Solberg, E. (2013). Location, education and enterprise growth. *Applied Economics Letters, 20*(10), 1019–1022. https://doi.org/10.1080/13504851.2013.772287

Hölzl, W. (2009). Is the R&D behaviour of fast-growing SMEs different? Evidence from CIS III data for 16 countries. *Small Business Economics, 33*, 59–75.

Hölzl, W. (2014). Persistence, survival, and growth: A closer look at 20 years of fast-growing firms in Austria. *Industrial and Corporate Change, 23*(1), 199–231. https://doi.org/10.1093/icc/dtt054

Jansen, J. J. P., Heavey, C., Mom, T. J. M., Simsek, Z., & Zahra, S. A. (2023). Scaling-up: Building, leading and sustaining rapid growth over time. *Journal of Management Studies, 60*(3), 581–604. https://doi.org/10.1111/joms.12910

Khurana, I. K., Martin, X., & Periera, R. (2008). Cross-listing and firm growth. *Review of Finance, 12*(2), 293–322. Scopus. https://doi.org/10.1093/rof/rfm031

Kubičková, V., Krošláková, M., Michálková, A., & Benešová, D. (2018). Gazelles in services: What are the specifics of their existence in Slovakia? *Management & Marketing, 13*(2), 929–945. https://doi.org/10.2478/mmcks-2018-0014

Landström, H. (2007). *Handbook of research on venture capital*. Edward Elgar Publishing. https://books.google.com/books?hl=pl&lr=&id=Rs60RxUoJeQC&oi=fnd&pg=

PR1&dq=Landstrom,+2007&ots=S7Thk5bKrg&sig=ZPiSeUHgh8c4iouegcDQ5OkQtGk

Le Roy, F., & Czakon, W. (2016). Managing coopetition: The missing link between strategy and performance. *Industrial Marketing Management, 53*(1), 3–6.

Levratto, N., Zouikri, M., & Tessier, L. (2010). The determinants of growth for smes-a longitudinal study from french manufacturing firms. *Available at SSRN 1780466.* https://papers.ssrn.com/sol3/papers.cfm?abstract_id=1780466

Lopez-Garcia, P., & Puente, S. (2012). What makes a high-growth firm? A dynamic probit analysis using Spanish firm-level data. *Small Business Economics, 39*(4), 1029–1041. https://doi.org/10.1007/s11187-011-9321-z

Majeed, O., Balaguer, A., Hansell, D., Hendrickson, L., Latcham, A., & Satherley, T. (2021). What drives high growth? Characteristics of Australian firms. *Economic Record, 97*(318), 350–364. https://doi.org/10.1111/1475-4932.12612

Mansikkamäki, S. (2023). Firm growth and profitability: The role of age and size in shifts between growth–profitability configurations. *Journal of Business Venturing Insights, 19*, e00372.

Mason, C., & Brown, R. (2010). *High growth firms in Scotland.* https://strathprints.strath.ac.uk/28232/

McKenzie, D. (2017). Identifying and spurring high-growth entrepreneurship: Experimental evidence from a business plan competition. *American Economic Review, 107*(8), 2278–2307.

Medovnikov, D. S., Rozmirovich, S. D., Oganesyan, T. K., Stepanov, A. K., & Mazurova, S. A. (2023). *Gazelle companies in the Russian economy: Innovation, steady rise, and crisis response*. https://dspace.spbu.ru/bitstream/11701/44336/1/02.pdf

Mohr, V., Garnsey, E., & Theyely, G. (2014). The role of alliances in the early development of high-growth firms. *Industrial and Corporate Change, 23*(1), 233–259. https://doi.org/10.1093/icc/dtt056

Monteiro, G. F. A. (2019). High-growth firms and scale-ups: A review and research agenda. *RAUSP Management Journal, 54*, 96–111.

Moschella, D., Tamagni, F., & Yu, X. (2019). Persistent high-growth firms in China's manufacturing. *Small Business Economics, 52*(3), 573–594. https://doi.org/10.1007/s11187-017-9973-4

OECD. (2009). *Regions matter economic recovery, innovation and sustainable growth.* OECD.

OECD. (2010). *High-Growth Enterprises: What governments can do to make a difference*. OECD Publishing.

OECD. (2016). *Entrepreneurship at a Glance 2016*. Organisation for Economic Co-operation and Development. https://www.oecd-ilibrary.org/industry-and-services/entrepreneurship-at-a-glance-2016_entrepreneur_aag-2016-en

OECD. (2021). *Understanding firm growth: Helping SMEs scale up*. OECD Publishing.

Oliner, S. D., Sichel, D. E., & Stiroh, K. J. (2008). Explaining a productive decade. *Journal of Policy Modeling, 30*(4), 633–673.

Orser, B., & Hogarth-Scott, S. (2002). Opting for growth: Gender dimensions of choosing enterprise development. *Canadian Journal of Administrative Sciences/Revue Canadienne Des Sciences de l'Administration, 19*(3), 284–300. https://doi.org/10.1111/j.1936-4490.2002.tb00273.x

Pereira, V., & Temouri, Y. (2018). Impact of institutions on emerging European high-growth firms. *Management Decision, 56*(1), 175–187. https://doi.org/10.1108/MD-03-2017-0279

Philippon, T., & Veron, N. (2008). *Financing Europe's Fast Movers. Bruegel Policy Brief 2008/01, January 2008*. https://aei.pitt.edu/id/eprint/8321

Rasmussen, C. C., Ladegård, G., & Korhonen-Sande, S. (2018). Growth intentions and board composition in high-growth firms. *Journal of Small Business Management, 56*(4), 601–617. https://doi.org/10.1111/jsbm.12307

Rasmussen, L. V., Fold, N., Olesen, R. S., & Shackleton, S. (2021). Socio-economic outcomes of ecological infrastructure investments. *Ecosystem Services, 47*, 101242. https://doi.org/10.1016/j.ecoser.2020.101242

Reyes, J.-D. (2017). Effects of FDI on high-growth firms in developing countries. *Global Investment Competitiveness Report 2017/2018*, 51.

Schreyer, P. (2000). *High-growth firms and employment*. OECD. https://doi.org/10.1787/861275538813

Sedlacek, P., & Ignaszak, M. (2021). *Productivity, profitability and growth*. https://papers.ssrn.com/sol3/papers.cfm?abstract_id=3886647

Senderovitz, M., Klyver, K., & Steffens, P. (2016). Four years on: Are the gazelles still running? A longitudinal study of firm performance after a period of rapid growth. *International Small Business Journal: Researching Entrepreneurship, 34*(4), 391–411. https://doi.org/10.1177/0266242614567483

Shepherd, D., & Wiklund, J. (2009). Are we comparing apples with apples or apples with oranges? Appropriateness of knowledge accumulation across growth studies. *Entrepreneurship Theory and Practice, 33*(1), 105–123. https://doi.org/10.1111/j.1540-6520.2008.00282.x

Sheppard, M. (2010). *Antecedents of high-growth and gazelle enterprises: An empirical study*. https://uwspace.uwaterloo.ca/handle/10012/5069

Shkolnykova, M. (2023). Assessing the importance of proximity dimensions for the diffusion of radical innovations in German biotechnology. *European Planning Studies, 31*(7), 1510–1531. https://doi.org/10.1080/09654313.2022.2147392

Shkolnykova, M., & Kudic, M. (2022). Who benefits from SMEs' radical innovations?—Empirical evidence from German biotechnology. *Small Business Economics, 58*(2), 1157–1185. https://doi.org/10.1007/s11187-021-00464-x

Širec, K., & Močnik, D. (Ed. Širec, K.) (2014). Gender-based differences in the performance of Slovenian high-growth companies. In *Women's entrepreneurship in the 21st century: An international multi-level research analysis*. Edward Elgar Publishing Ltd, 165–185. https://doi.org/10.4337/9781782544616.00016

Sleuwaegen, L., & Ramboer, S. (2020). Regional competitiveness and high growth firms in the EU: The creativity premium. *Applied Economics, 52*(22), 2325–2338. https://doi.org/10.1080/00036846.2019.1686454

Smallbone, D., Leig, R., & North, D. (1995). The characteristics and strategies of high growth SMEs. *International Journal of Entrepreneurial Behavior & Research, 1*(3), 44–62.

Solmon, L. C. (2019). *Labor markets, employment policy, and job creation*. Routledge.

Spitsin, V., Vuković, D. B., Ryzhkova, M., & Leonova, V. (2024). Pathways to prosperity: Navigating post-stagnation growth and revitalizing business. *Economies, 12*(3), 55.

Spitsin, V., Vukovic, D., Mikhalchuk, A., Spitsina, L., & Novoseltseva, D. (2023). High-tech gazelle firms at various stages of evolution: Performance and distinctive features. *Journal of Economic Studies, 50*(4), 674–695.

Srhoj, S. (2022). Can we predict high growth firms with financial ratios? *Financial Internet Quarterly, 18*(1), 66–73. https://doi.org/10.2478/fiqf-2022-0006

Stam, E. (2010). Growth beyond Gibrat: Firm growth processes and strategies. *Small Business Economics*, *35*(2), 129–135. https://doi.org/10.1007/s11187-010-9294-3

Stam, E., & Van De Ven, A. (2021). Entrepreneurial ecosystem elements. *Small Business Economics*, *56*(2), 809–832. https://doi.org/10.1007/s11187-019-00270-6

Stam, E., & Wennberg, K. (2009). The roles of R&D in new firm growth. *Small Business Economics*, *33*(1), 77–89. https://doi.org/10.1007/s11187-009-9183-9

Sterk, V., Sedláček, P., & Pugsley, B. (2021). The nature of firm growth. *American Economic Review*, *111*(2), 547–579. https://doi.org/10.1257/AER.20190748

Storey, D. (2001). *A Portrait of Success: The Facts Behind High Growth Companies in the UK (Deloitte & Touche, London)*. https://dbc.wroc.pl/Content/40106/PDF/SiM%20451%20Zygmunt%20druk%2017_03_20_POPR.pdf

Teruel, M., & De Wit, G. (2011). Determinants of high-growth firms. *Why Have Some Countries More High-Growth Firms than Others*. https://www.researchgate.net/profile/Mercedes-Teruel/publication/241756936_Determinants_of_high-growth_firms/links/5405e0320cf2c48563b1db80/Determinants-of-high-growth-firms.pdf

Tomenendal, M., & Raffer, C. (2023). *Where do gazelles and high-growth firms occur in Germany?* BPS Working Paper. https://www.econstor.eu/handle/10419/273484

Wajsman, N., Kazimierczak, M., Ménière, Y., & Rudyk, I. (2019). *High-growth firms and intellectual property rights*. EUIPO.

Weinblat, J. (2018). Forecasting European high-growth firms—A random forest approach. *Journal of Industry, Competition and Trade*, *18*(3), 253–294. https://doi.org/10.1007/s10842-017-0257-0

Young, G., Smith, K. G., & Grimm, C. M. (1996). "Austrian" and industrial organization perspectives on firm-level competitive activity and performance. *Organization Science*, *7*(3), 243–254. https://doi.org/10.1287/orsc.7.3.243

Zhou, H., & De Wit, G. (2009). Determinants and dimensions of firm growth. *Scales EIM Research Reports (H200903)*. https://papers.ssrn.com/sol3/papers.cfm?abstract_id=1443897

2 The concept of entrepreneurial ecosystems and sustainable high growth

2.1 The core of entrepreneurial ecosystems

In light of ambiguous research findings regarding resource-based factors of growth, as discussed in Chapter 1, the latest research on determinants of expansion focuses on the environment in a systemic perspective, as reflected in the concept of entrepreneurial ecosystems (EEs, Isenberg, 2011; Mason & Brown, 2014; Spigel, 2017). Spatial elements in entrepreneurship research have gained popularity relatively recently (Baker & Welter, 2020). It has been widely recognized that entrepreneurs are not able to manage all the resources needed for the functioning of an enterprise, particularly those related to the economic environment. EEs are considered one of the most important concepts of the last decade in the field of entrepreneurship support policy and regional development (Spigel et al., 2020). The concept emerged during a period of economic stagnation triggered, among other things, by the 2007–2009 crisis, which, given the limited effectiveness of earlier theories and development policies, contributed to its rapid popularization (Spigel et al., 2020).

There is no single strict definition of an EE. Cohen (2006) defined the EE as *"a group of interrelated actors in a local geographic community who are committed to sustainable development through supporting and facilitating new sustainable ventures"* (Alvedalen & Boschma, 2017). Acs (2014) defined the EE (National System of Entrepreneurship) as *"dynamic, institutionally embedded interactions between entrepreneurial attitudes, abilities and aspirations of individuals, which drive the allocation of resources through the creation and operation of new ventures."* According to Stam (2016), an EE is *"a set of interdependent actors and factors coordinated in such a way that they enable productive entrepreneurship."* Another definition was provided by Qian (2013), according to whom an EE (system of entrepreneurship) is *"the economic, social, institutional and all other relevant factors that interactively influence the creation, discovery and exploitation of entrepreneurial opportunities."*

DOI: 10.4324/9781003739333-3

Spigel (2017), in turn, holds that an EE is *"a combination of local cultural outlooks, social networks, investment capital, universities, and active economic policies that create environments supportive of innovation-based ventures."*

EEs are complex phenomena that emerge as a result of the actions of individuals (Spigel, 2017). Since economic activity involves interactions with other actors, the essence of an ecosystem lies in interactions. Isenberg (2010) understands EEs as *"a set of interconnected elements such as leadership, culture, capital, markets, human resource skills, and support that foster the development of entrepreneurship."* The use of network theory to describe EEs is also popular, as this theory is considered key in entrepreneurship research (Purbasari et al., 2020; Spigel, 2017). Consequently to this network focus, EEs are regarded as a concept of economic policy that represents a reconceptualization and development of cluster-based policies and measures.

This study adopts a definition of EEs that follows the approach of Stam and Van De Ven (2021) and integrates the discussed views, treating "*entrepreneurial ecosystems as sets of interdependent actors and resources that generate productive entrepreneurship within a specific territory.*" EEs thus constitute a concept of a systemic, functionally oriented environment of enterprises within a defined geographic area (region, country).

Due to their dynamic nature, EEs are described using evolutionary economics (Dosi et al., 2020). Evolutionary concepts of EEs assume that EEs change over time and evolve. Depending on their structural characteristics, these systems may exhibit different levels of effectiveness in generating productive entrepreneurship (Brown et al., 2017; Mack & Mayer, 2016). Evolutionary processes increase diversity within the ecosystem and lead to its stability (Roundy et al., 2017). Still, little is known about the mechanisms governing the evolution of EEs (Alvedalen & Boschma, 2017).

The evolution of an ecosystem is modeled on biological mechanisms, where a primary ecosystem without life and nutrients is gradually colonized by pioneers, and the subsequent growth of resources leads to the succession of new species and the formation of a complex ecosystem with a high degree of interconnections among the species that compose it. Ecosystem stability is threatened by external shocks and a potential collapse, after which the cycle begins anew (Auerswald & Dani, 2017). The biological concept of ecosystems can easily be translated into economic terms. The pioneers are replaced by the first entrepreneurs who, due to low competition, have easier access to resources. As new firms emerge, competition for resources intensifies, and the relationships formed between companies lead to the establishment of equilibrium. This persists until a sudden change occurs, forcing less stable firms to close, which leads to a reconfiguration of the ecosystem, resulting in a new ecosystem different from the previous one (Auerswald & Dani, 2017). Mack and Mayer (2016) proposed a four-phase model, described in more detail in the subsection concerning the role of EEs in economic policy.

Often, the concept of entrepreneurship in EEs is reduced to support for high-growth firms, which are a key theme in entrepreneurship research (Stam & Van De Ven, 2021). Some researchers even argue that EEs are a concept designed specifically to support fast-growing firms (Spigel et al., 2020). Although most research focuses on commercial organizations, the concept of EEs is not limited to for-profit firms and may also be successfully applied to non-profit organizations and other public benefit organizations (Roundy, 2017; Stam & Van De Ven, 2021). Current research is conducted mainly at an aggregated level, and the impact of EEs on individual firms remains relatively underexplored (Stam & Van De Ven, 2021).

The concept of an EE has a geographical scope (Roundy, 2017). Its boundaries are often based on administrative divisions and constrained by data availability. Researchers point out problems with accessing data at levels lower than the national level, while according to the concept of EEs, the regional or local scale is more natural (Spigel et al., 2020). Moreover, difficulties arise not only in terms of data availability but also in a variety of measurements; examples include entrepreneurial culture, the density of social networks, or the number of business angels. For quantitative indicators, there are proxy measures based on surveys; however, these are subjective measures, limited by respondents' opinions (Spigel et al., 2020). Therefore, the concept of EEs is often criticized for the lack of consistency when defining ecosystem boundaries and measuring it (Colombelli et al., 2019).

Another ambiguity regarding the boundaries of the phenomenon concerns the "regionality" of ecosystem components. Research so far has been conducted at the national level, administrative units, cities, and even parts of cities, such as university campuses. The elements of ecosystems presented in research as supporting entrepreneurship are factors that were previously studied without spatial limitations. Moreover, their multitude makes it difficult to establish cause-and-effect relationships (Alvedalen & Boschma, 2017). The geographical and regional context of EEs is convincing based on the relationship between entrepreneurship and regional development. Distance also plays a key role in the mobility of capital and knowledge spillovers, which are more evident within regions than between them. Knowledge spillover effects are thus defined by regional boundaries and have a local impact that weakens with geographical distance. Qian (2018) notes that knowledge spillovers lead to innovation and the formation of clusters, which supports the economic development of a region. While research on knowledge spillovers and other spatial effects is quite common, there is a research gap regarding their impact on EEs.

The idea of EE is one of the concepts of regional entrepreneurship development. It shares certain features with the concepts of regional innovation systems and clusters (Spigel, 2017). All these theories are based on the assumption that a significant part of a firm's competitive advantage can be explained by the regional environment, which consists of both material resources (e.g. infrastructure) and immaterial resources and processes, such as networks of cooperation between enterprises and knowledge transfer effects between universities and businesses (Spigel, 2017). However, in each of these concepts, different mechanisms shape competitive advantage. In the concepts of clusters and regional innovation systems, competitive advantage arises from localization benefits that allow firms to use the same resources, thereby reducing unit costs. By cooperating, firms can handle larger orders and exchange knowledge to increase production efficiency (Spigel, 2017). These benefits occur mainly within the same industry (Auerswald & Dani, 2017; Spigel, 2017). In EEs, by contrast, competitive advantage comes from the diffusion of knowledge (Spigel, 2017).

2.2 Structure of EEs

EEs have a systemic and spatial character, meaning they are based on the interdependencies of actors and resources within a defined territory (Acs et al., 2014, 2017; Brown & Mawson, 2019; Mason & Brown, 2014). The actors and resources of an ecosystem are often considered in such dimensions as institutional, financial, human, and social capital, material infrastructure, and research and development (R&D) infrastructure (Stam & Van De Ven, 2021). These dimensions are not a simple collection but interact with each other as a system. Furthermore, the selection of dimensions and their descriptive factors depends on the conceptualization of productive entrepreneurship (Spigel, 2017).

Research on the structure of ecosystems occupies an important place in the development of this concept. In EE, several to a dozen or so dimensions (elements, components, and pillars) are distinguished, each of which can be described using thematically related variables (Foster et al., 2013; Gancarczyk & Konopa, 2021). Initial research on the influence of territorial factors on entrepreneurship assumed that individual dimensions exert independent effects, although their nature is complex and they are interrelated.

Empirical analyses have made it possible to distinguish two basic approaches to identifying the components of an EE. According to the first approach, researchers describe general frameworks of dimensions that make up EE. For example, practitioners and some researchers distinguish such key components of an EE as the environment, consisting of the business environment and investment climate, interconnected actors, and an evolving culture and attitudes (Kreuzer et al., 2018). Another example is one of the first attempts to conceptualize the dimensions of ecosystems proposed by Van de Ven. He distinguished three elements, which he called *infrastructure*, namely, the institutional infrastructure regulating entrepreneurial activity, public resources available to firms, and the economic activity of entrepreneurs.

Over time, an increasing number of more detailed dimensions have been distinguished, and there is no consensus among researchers regarding the basic pillars on which the ecosystem is based. However, certain key components recur across a range of studies, including entrepreneurs, employees, investors, mentors, supportive legal regulations, the presence of research universities, and an entrepreneurial culture that encourages risk-taking. These components can generally be divided into material, social, and cultural categories (Spigel, 2017). Often, the ultimate selection of dimensions is limited by data availability.

For the development of the ecosystem, the presence of both large firms and small- and medium-sized enterprises is important. Large firms represent a significant segment of clients for more advanced technologies. The existence of substantial consumers of goods and services can incentivize large companies to locate in a given region, especially in industries with high transportation costs or where business services are less accessible (Foster et al., 2013). Furthermore, the presence of large corporations attracts skilled labor, which is trained within these firms, thereby increasing the overall skill level in society. The share of small entrepreneurs among all firms may be significant in certain industries (Gnyawali & Fogel, 1994). For example, in Poland, there are sectors such as the food industry where small entrepreneurs cannot compete on cost with market leaders, and opportunities to leverage other competitive advantages are limited. Moreover, diversification of economic activity can determine the competitiveness of the economic ecosystem. In regions with highly diversified economic activity, a wide range of goods and services is available from local firms, which should reduce the need to import them from other locations (Gnyawali & Fogel, 1994). Another important factor of EE development is the presence of loyal customers (businesses or individuals), which ensures revenue continuity in the medium and long term, providing firms with a sense of stability (Mungila Hillemane, 2020). Below, we present a narrative literature review to identify the core elements of EE for further empirical investigation, based on the existing research.

Human resource competencies

A frequently highlighted dimension of EE is human resource competencies, which encompass the general and vocational education and experience of the population. Entrepreneurial success is largely determined by the competencies of personnel. The inflow of foreign labor helps supplement human capital and prevents its rapid depletion amid the fast expansion of the EE (Foster et al., 2013). Attention is also drawn to the significant role of immigrants as a source of entrepreneurship, as well as advisors, mentors, and capital providers (Mungila Hillemane, 2020). The possibility of outsourcing skilled employees (e.g., lawyers or accountants) significantly reduces costs for firms (Foster et al., 2013). Talented managers can accelerate firm growth, which should positively impact the success of EEs (Foster et al., 2013).

Sources of financing

An important element of the ecosystem is access to debt and equity financing. Sources of capital may include business angels or banks that offer loans (Foster et al., 2013). Low capital acquisition costs are also important, as they stimulate the search for external funding. Competition among financial firms leads to lower financing costs. Public credit guarantee programs for new enterprises facilitate their start; equally important is a supportive approach from private financial institutions (Gnyawali & Fogel, 1994).

Over 25% of newly created enterprises rely on financial support from family and friends, and more than 65% use their own savings (Liguori et al., 2019). Therefore, when assessing financing conditions within an EE, the wealth of the society should be taken into account. General wealth can also influence the success of less common financing strategies such as crowdfunding. Research shows that the source of a firm's financing can have varying effects on its survival, depending on the stage of development of the EE (Clayton et al., 2023).

Knowledge development and R&D

Access to knowledge and R&D development builds a foundation for innovations and the competitive advantage of firms. The infusion of knowledge and support for R&D are offered by the universities, technology parks, innovation centers, technology incubators, and accelerators (Roundy, 2017). Incubators aim to support entrepreneurs in the early stages of their operations by providing consulting services and office space. They also offer comprehensive support in the form of legal and accounting services (Deyanova et al., 2022). Accelerators, on the other hand, usually run mentoring programs and provide financial support for specific development projects in exchange for equity in the venture.

Access to mentorship and consultations contributes to the development of knowledge and R&D activities (Foster et al., 2013). Firms receiving external consulting performed better in less developed countries, whereas entrepreneurs in the USA consider advisory support to be of limited importance. Consulting firms can also substitute for mentors (Gnyawali & Fogel, 1994). Technology incubators are important as intermediaries between startups and established companies (Blanka & Traunmüller, 2020).

The entrepreneurs' associations facilitate networking within the same or different industries (Foster et al., 2013). In addition to formal associations, informal networks shape the culture of collaboration within the EE. Formal entrepreneurial networks can support entrepreneurs by reducing the risk of business failure (Hoang & Antoncic, 2003). The greatest advantage of networks, however, is the access to information and knowledge of their participants (Hoang & Antoncic, 2003). Membership in formal networks can also improve a firm's reputation (Hoang & Antoncic, 2003). Companies with significant strategic partners increase their market value more rapidly, and international partners enhance foreign expansion. Network membership benefits firms of all ages, although established companies may have different expectations from those of young firms (Johannisson et al., 1994; Johannisson & Mønsted, 1997). Participation in formal networks often strengthens informal relationships between firms.

Knowledge development through education appears in nearly all proposed components of EEs. Promoting entrepreneurial education and training through universities and providers of business services strengthens the culture of entrepreneurship in a region (Foster et al., 2013). Training allows entrepreneurs to fill gaps in education and skills that are particularly relevant to them (Gnyawali & Fogel, 1994). Research also shows that entrepreneurial education positively influences entrepreneurial intentions and the internationalization of firms. Education not only supports business creation but also increases the likelihood of business survival (Mackiewicz & Kurczewska, 2023).

However, the role of universities is not limited to education. Higher education and R&D institutions are primary sources of technical knowledge flow (Matt & Schaeffer, 2018). Universities play a significant role in the evolution of EEs, particularly as a seed for their formation, serving as creators of knowledge (Novela et al., 2021). Higher education and research institutions also frequently participate in clusters, which can attract knowledge-seeking firms from abroad (Goetz, 2006).

Digital economy

Digital activities are increasingly determining various types of business. Operating in digital markets allows companies to attract more customers, especially younger ones. The main channels of impact are an increase in the customer base and better access to financing (Hassna, 2022). The Internet is also the primary source where entrepreneurs seek information, including information on business support institutions.

Traditional EEs have been integrating with their digital counterparts across multiple dimensions. The digital ecosystem provides many entrepreneurial opportunities, and its role increased during the COVID-19 pandemic (Purbasari et al., 2021). For this reason, other authors include the digital economy in assessments of EE performance (Koroleva, 2022; Torres & Godinho, 2022) and in their dimensions. Internet access is sometimes considered part of the infrastructure dimension. However, equating digitalization solely with infrastructure is not justified. The digital economy dimension has specific characteristics related to technology and skills and is not limited to telecommunication infrastructure.

Physical infrastructure and natural environment

Another important element of the EE is physical structure. Access to land, facilities, electricity, water, and high-speed Internet is a crucial development condition (Foster et al., 2013). Efficient transport infrastructure is also essential (Gnyawali & Fogel, 1994). Poorly developed infrastructure is one of the most frequently reported barriers to entrepreneurship and is considered a significant obstacle to economic development. Investing in infrastructure in less developed countries has a multiplier effect on the economy by increasing inter-regional linkages and stimulating trade and economic connections (Mohmand et al., 2021).

The natural environment is relatively rarely highlighted as a dimension of the EE. Two main aspects are typically emphasized. The first concerns the presence of natural resources within the ecosystem, which can serve as a development driver, particularly in less developed regions (Suresh & Ramraj, 2012). However, in the developed countries, EEs can emerge even in the absence of natural resources, as exemplified by Japan. The second aspect concerns climate. Countries prone to extreme events are perceived as less attractive for investment due to the high costs of protecting against natural disasters. There are documented cases of firms relocating due to climate-related reasons (Mungila Hillemane, 2020). Human physiology is also adapted to specific ranges of temperature and humidity, and exceeding these ranges reduces productivity. For this reason, investors may avoid regions with excessively low or high temperatures.

Institutions

Institutions encompass sets of formal and informal rules, norms, and regulations that govern human activity and affect transaction costs. Legal regulations are a key component of EEs. Simple procedures for starting a business encourage potential entrepreneurs to launch ventures and experiment with new ideas. In addition, low taxes and tax exemptions contribute to entrepreneurial activity (Foster et al., 2013). Progressive taxation negatively impacts economic activity and discourages business creation. The level of taxation is also considered by firms planning to establish foreign branches and is treated as an element of regional competitiveness. Moreover, the relationship between labor taxation and business taxation is important. High labor taxes may push people toward self-employment (Simón-Moya et al., 2014). Import and export restrictions effectively limit international activity, although uncertainty regarding import restrictions can stimulate innovation (Gnyawali & Fogel, 1994).

Cultural factors are important but relatively under-researched elements influencing entrepreneurship (Foster et al., 2013; Gancarczyk et al., 2023). Higher levels of entrepreneurship occur in communities that promote social cooperation, whereas societies with a strong individualistic culture tend to have lower entrepreneurial activity. Risk tolerance and acceptance of failure are additional culturally conditioned factors that influence entrepreneurship (Foster et al., 2013). In countries where entrepreneurs are socially stigmatized after failure, entrepreneurial activity is lower. Moreover, a previous business failure can hinder access to investment for subsequent ventures. Societal preferences regarding income generation and the positive image of entrepreneurs also influence the number of new firms created. This effect can aggregate at the regional level (Foster et al., 2013). Promoting innovation within the ecosystem community may foster entrepreneurial initiatives (Foster et al., 2013).

The presence of experienced entrepreneurs who serve as role models can guide the development of firms within the ecosystem. Citizens' engagement is another important factor affecting entrepreneurship. Membership in non-profit organizations and social activity strengthens collaboration skills, which are essential for entrepreneurial success. Broad social networks facilitate the identification of community imbalances and help achieve consensus within the community (Mandrysz, 2020).

Entrepreneurial culture is a rather difficult category to measure. To determine its level, both qualitative and quantitative methods are used (Stam & Van De Ven, 2021). The dominant religion within an ecosystem influences business conditions. In Islamic countries, entrepreneurship is considered a typically male activity, so businesses run by women in ecosystems where this culture prevails may face discrimination (Tlaiss & McAdam, 2021). A less frequently highlighted component of ecosystem culture is the mental (moral) culture, which determines the role of the entrepreneurs' immediate family in supporting their businesses. In particular, this concerns the willingness to establish family businesses within a given ecosystem and the inclination of parents to start businesses to improve work-time flexibility (Suresh & Ramraj, 2012).

An analysis of the principal components in 10 regions of the Netherlands and 16 regions of Poland revealed that the dimensions of EEs can be reduced to one to two leading dimensions, indicating a high correlation among the included factors (Gancarczyk & Konopa, 2021; Stam & Van De Ven, 2021). Not all pillars of EEs contribute to firm growth in the opinion of entrepreneurs, and their subjective perceptions may not align with objective regional growth factors (Foster et al., 2013).

EEs differ in dimension configurations, but not all dimensions have similar discriminative power when attempting to group ecosystems with structurally similar characteristics. For example, taxes and bureaucracy, material infrastructure, and internal market regulations demonstrate low significance, while internal market dynamics do not influence the grouping of EEs in Arab countries, according to a study conducted by Davari and Najmabadi in Iran (Davari & Najmabadi, 2018).

2.3 Sustainable high growth of enterprises as an outcome of EEs

Currently, the idea of productive entrepreneurship has become a central element of the concept of EEs (Nicotra et al., 2018; Wurth et al., 2022). Research in this field is at an early stage and is most often qualitative in nature. Quantitative analyses are rare, and their results regarding the impact of EEs on productive entrepreneurship remain inconclusive (Acs et al., 2014, 2017). This is related to the incomplete conceptualization of productive growth, as well as differing views on the EE dimensions in terms of their sufficiency and necessity for achieving expected outcomes (Stam & Van De Ven, 2021). Productive entrepreneurship is most often associated with high-growth enterprises, although other interpretations also exist (e.g., GDP, the number of firms or startups).

According to W. Baumol (1990, 1994), productive entrepreneurship is "[…] *activity that directly or indirectly contributes to increasing economic outcomes, or to increasing the possibilities of achieving additional outcomes.*" Foss (1996) emphasizes the role of productive entrepreneurship in entrepreneurial discoveries, which contribute to increasing the overall surplus. Productive entrepreneurship leads to progress and economic growth. A productive entrepreneur introduces technological advancement through innovation and discovers new opportunities for generating income, leading to economic development.

Productive entrepreneurship is influenced by efficiently functioning economic institutions (e.g., private property and capital markets), political institutions (e.g., fiscal and monetary policy and transparency), and legal institutions (e.g., effective courts). Inefficient institutions lead to unproductive entrepreneurship (Sobel, 2008). Unproductive entrepreneurship does not provide economic and social values, and its only goal is profit. Entrepreneurs seeking profit may evade taxes and engage in other unethical practices (Lucas & Fuller, 2017). Unproductive entrepreneurship provides value for the entrepreneurs themselves but does not create aggregated net value (Baumol, 1996). It does not improve economic outcomes and manifests as opportunism, corruption, resource waste, pursuit of political rent, or activities in the informal economy (Brixiova, 2010; Sobel, 2008). In recent years, a relative decline in unproductive entrepreneurship has been observed, attributed to legal reforms, yet the problem remains relevant. This raises the question of whether and how EEs can stimulate productive entrepreneurship and overall societal well-being (Spigel et al., 2020).

The essence of productive entrepreneurship lies in creating added value not only for the entrepreneur but also for the economy and society. Productive entrepreneurship increases societal well-being and has a sustainable and lasting character, contributing economic, social, and environmental value. Productive entrepreneurship is often associated with productive firm growth, which generates economic value through rapid growth. This growth is usually based on the implementation of innovations, which not only stimulate organizational expansion but also replace technologically and morally outdated solutions, due to their impact on quality of life and the natural environment.

Productive entrepreneurship also brings social value by creating high-value-added jobs, which is linked to the knowledge intensity of the activity. Sometimes, this is referred to as the social efficiency of firms (Zbierowski, 2021). Finally, productive entrepreneurship should be characterized by durability, in the sense of the ability to avoid failure and lost investments, and therefore should demonstrate economic efficiency, which can be expressed through profitability.

In light of the above, it is justified *to conceptualize productive entrepreneurship as sustainable high growth (SHG), that is, high growth that delivers economic and social value. The SHG concept integrates the ideas of productive entrepreneurship and rapid firm growth, expressing fast expansion that combines economic efficiency with social value in the form of employment growth.*

So defined, SHG does not depend on a single factor but on multiple dimensions of the environment (Baumol, 1996; Baumol et al., 1994; Brixiova, 2010; Sobel, 2008). Little is known about the impact of specific ecosystem dimensions on SHG. The dimensions of an ecosystem are partially substitutive, and certain gaps may be compensated by other pillars. However, it remains unclear to what extent these gaps affect productive entrepreneurship (Schrijvers et al., 2024; Spigel, 2017). Moreover, the effect of EEs may vary depending on the characteristics of the enterprise (Alam et al., 2023).

The effectiveness of EEs has been a topic of growing interest over the past decade (Tapsi & Baga, 2024). The number of studies in this area is rising, with 60% of articles published in the last three years (Tapsi & Baga, 2024). This surge in interest is driven by the search for sources of economic growth, and the link between entrepreneurship and economic development is recognized not only by researchers but also by leading policymakers (Isenberg, 2010). Therefore, there is a need to define metrics that allow for the assessment of EE effectiveness.

Stam and Van De Ven (2021) note that the relationship between EEs and productive entrepreneurship is bidirectional: EEs generate productive entrepreneurship, but on the other hand, in regions where businesses perform well, EEs are likely to be well-developed. In Stam and Van De Ven's (2021) article, the indicator of productive entrepreneurship was the share of fast-growing firms in the ecosystem. The coefficient of determination was 0.437, indicating a fairly strong dependence between the quality of the EE and the share of fast-growing firms (Stam & Van De Ven, 2021). The share of fast-growing firms in a region also showed some temporal correlation (Stam & Van De Ven, 2021).

Nicotra distinguished three primary measures of productive entrepreneurship that can be applied to SHG as well, that is, entrepreneurial activity, innovation, and outcomes (Nicotra et al., 2018). The number of new firms is sometimes used to measure the outcomes of EEs, although some researchers treat this indicator as inadequate (Leendertse et al., 2022). Since SHG creates added value, it is argued that the number of new innovative firms is a better proxy (Leendertse et al., 2022). The share of firms surviving five years can also serve as a reflection of EE performance, highlighting the ecosystem's friendliness toward new firms. The proportion of people planning to start a business and those who started a business no more than 3.5 years earlier is an example of other measures (Kansheba, 2020). A disadvantage of this measurement method is the necessity of conducting surveys. Monitoring the development of entrepreneurial intentions requires panel data analyses, but due to panel attrition, studies must use methods to mitigate this issue (e.g., rotational panels), which makes them time-consuming and costly.

The volume of foreign direct investment and the size of innovation exports are sometimes used as indicators of EE performance at the international level. However, these measures have not gained significant acceptance among researchers or practitioners and are therefore rarely used (Kreuzer et al., 2018). Other measures include labor productivity growth, employment growth, the number of gazelles, the share of firms with a scalable business model, and the number of unicorns, although the latter appears only in highly developed ecosystems, and is not widely promoted due to its rarity (Acs et al., 2017). Torres emphasizes that not only unicorns but also digitally active unicorns matter, highlighting the importance of innovation (Torres & Godinho, 2022).

Innovation is a general category that can also reflect the EE performance. Since the process of creating innovations is nonlinear and only some ideas advance to subsequent stages, an innovation-based ecosystem performance indicator can include three components of the innovation process: the number of generated ideas, the number of ideas that entered the development phase, and the percentage of commercialized innovations. Measuring innovation at the regional level is important because breakthrough innovations arise not at the level of individual firms but of regions, as a result of the activities of many mutually supporting actors. Strong EEs contribute to enhancing innovation both at the regional level and within individual firms.

Previous studies have been conducted using regional data to describe and evaluate EEs. Some researchers also distinguish EEs within specific industries, allowing for a more focused measurement of outcomes. For example, in studies of ecosystems supporting FinTech in Russia – which has one of the largest FinTech development indices – the EE was evaluated on the number of registered firms in this industry (Koroleva, 2022).

There are two main approaches to constructing indicators of EE development: additive and multiplicative. Additive indicators tend to flatten differences in development levels compared to multiplicative indicators, which highlight these differences (Leendertse et al., 2022). Some researchers also use log-transformed variables to reduce the range of calculated indicators

(Leendertse et al., 2022). Most metrics use a single variable as a measure of ecosystem performance. However, a composite index can more comprehensively reflect the level of productive entrepreneurship. Lubis constructed a synthetic index based on four variables: innovative start-ups, the number of venture capital-backed start-ups, the number of unicorns, and start-ups developing opportunity-based entrepreneurship (Lubis et al., 2023). In another study, the impact of EEs on firms' financial performance was analyzed. For this purpose, a four-element synthetic indicator was also used: percentage growth in profits, percentage growth in gross financial result, gross turnover profitability ratio, and percentage growth of first-degree financial liquidity (Gancarczyk & Konopa, 2021).

EEs vary significantly in terms of their characteristics and performance (Schrijvers et al., 2024). Several research gaps exist in this area. There is a scarcity of studies on which dimensions of EEs influence outcome indicators (Gancarczyk et al., 2025). Moreover, due to the use of aggregated data, previous research lacks analyses of the heterogeneous effects of dimensions on structurally similar firms. It is also unclear whether EEs affect all firms equally, or whether this impact is moderated by the heterogeneous characteristics of the firms.

As indicated above, EE performance and SHG can be measured in a variety of ways. It can be assumed that EEs should influence SHG, but different dimensions may have different effects on this complex outcome. Furthermore, firms exhibit significant heterogeneity in their resources and regional contexts (Cattaruzzo & Teruel, 2022; Neubaum et al., 2019). Certain factors influence entrepreneurial intentions and the number of firms founded, others have a significant impact on innovativeness, and still others on firm growth. Unicorns appear to be unique and absent in most ecosystems, and their presence requires particularly demanding conditions. SHG may depend on a specific combination of EE dimensions with varying characteristics. Based on the review of the essence, characteristics, and effects of EEs on SHG, we formulate Hypotheses 1, 2, and 2.1.

H1. *Sustainable high growth of enterprises depends on the structural characteristics of entrepreneurial ecosystems.*

H2. *The influence of entrepreneurial ecosystems on the sustainable high growth of firms is moderated by the heterogeneity of the companies operating within these ecosystems.*

H2.1. *The influence of entrepreneurial ecosystems on the sustainable high growth of enterprises is moderated by enterprise characteristics such as age, size, scope of operations, and knowledge intensity of their activities.*

Furthermore, as discussed above, research on HGE predominantly concentrates on size dynamics, overlooking effects in terms of expected profitability, which is one of the conditions for long-term survival (resilience, resistance to market changes) and for avoiding failure and resource waste. The same research gap can be found in the EE studies that treat high-growth entrepreneurship as an expected outcome; namely, they emphasize the size dynamics rather than performance and resilience (Stam & Van De Ven, 2021; Wurth et al., 2022). However, it can be assumed that firms that achieved productive growth in the preceding period are better able to leverage a given EE due to their developed resources (McKelvie & Wiklund, 2010). Companies that have experienced previous growth generally continue to expand (McKelvie & Wiklund, 2010; Penrose, 1959). On this basis, we formulate hypothesis 2.2:

H2.2. *Prior sustainable high growth of enterprises moderates the impact of entrepreneurial ecosystems on future sustainable high growth of these enterprises.*

The assumptions included in the hypotheses 1 and 2 will further guide our empirical research design in Chapter 3.

2.4 EEs in economic policy

The concept of EE is attractive from the perspective of economic policy because it focuses on creating a system – an engaged community and resources linked to entrepreneurship – rather than merely investing in infrastructure (Spigel et al., 2020). However, a significant challenge is the process of EE formation and the design of adequate economic policy measures (Gnyawali & Fogel, 1994). Although the individual dimensions of EEs have been studied, gaps remain in understanding the mechanisms of regulation (governance) that enable the establishment and development of the EE (Colombelli et al., 2019). Governance allows for more efficient utilization of ecosystems for economic policy purposes. For example, the development of EEs contributes to increased innovation and job creation, which should enhance overall societal well-being (Spigel et al., 2020). A well-functioning EE is also desirable from the perspective of societal wealth, and politicians seeking to improve it can gain recognition from voters.

Implementing EEs is a complex process and often does not proceed smoothly. Decision-makers make many mistakes, the most significant of which is focusing on one or two components of the ecosystem (Isenberg, 2010). EEs are a set of interrelated elements and are not always treated holistically in economic policy design (Isenberg, 2010). Decision-makers should also avoid attempting to replicate other ecosystems, as these arise through evolution and are a product of the overall local context (Cho et al., 2022; Isenberg, 2010). Therefore, economic policy should be based on the local entrepreneurial culture, which in different regions favors different styles of conducting businesses (Isenberg, 2010).

The legal environment and administrative procedures are crucial for supporting EEs. At the same time, these elements are often the main focus of politicians because legal changes are easier to implement compared to other systemic changes (Isenberg, 2010). The ability to implement legal reforms largely depends on the characteristics of the country. In Poland, most laws defining rights and obligations for business activity are enacted at the level of the parliament (acts), government, and president (regulations). Although other authorities are also empowered to issue regulations, their significance is minor. Local governments and executive bodies at various administrative levels have much less influence on the legal sphere, and their local legal acts must not contradict higher-level laws. Consequently, there is little variation in legal conditions across Polish EEs.

However, local governments can support entrepreneurship by setting local taxes and fees or defining criteria for exemptions. Exemption criteria are primarily subject-based, aiming to promote specific types of activities (Pietkun, 2024). Spatial planning can significantly affect possible business locations. Poorly designed location restrictions, requirements for usable floor area, and landscape protection can discourage entrepreneurs from operating in a region. On the other hand, regional authorities have at their disposal various instruments from national programs and economic organizations (in Poland, EU programs) when preparing regional development plans. It is also important to prioritize interventions. Not all problems affecting ecosystems impact them equally. Informed decision-makers should identify which solutions will bring the most benefits in the short term and assign them the highest priority. To determine these priorities, consultations with key ecosystem actors should be conducted.

In recent years, there have been attempts to transfer strategic management concepts from firms to regions. According to this approach, EEs should be managed comprehensively and possess a long-term development strategy based on their specific resources (Audretsch & Belitski, 2017). Planning the development of an EE, particularly strategic development, requires taking into account the phase of the ecosystem's evolution. In the Mack and Mayer (2016) model, during the first phase of EE evolution, there are few firms, and the birth rate of firms exceeds the mortality rate. At this stage, decision-makers' activities focus on traditional aspects: clusters, firm retention, and enhancing the region's attractiveness to attract new firms. Opportunities for financing are limited at this stage, and key ecosystem dimensions are still underdeveloped to sustain a fully functioning ecosystem. Entrepreneurship incubators and non-profit foundations also develop slowly during this phase.

In the second phase of EE evolution, more new firms are established than those that exit the market. During this phase, policymakers begin to recognize the existence of the EE and start directing regional policies toward entrepreneurship development, while capital becomes more accessible to firms. Universities start offering entrepreneurship education, which gradually penetrates local mentalities and leads to the emergence of the first serial entrepreneurs.

In the stability phase, which is the third phase of EE development, the growth of new enterprises slows, and the firm mortality rate begins to exceed new firm creation. The main reason for this is the rising cost of market entry. Salaries offered by firms may become more attractive than potential earnings as an entrepreneur. This phase is crucial for EEs because only regional policies focused on supporting entrepreneurship can maintain the ecosystem.

The final phase is the decline of the EE, characterized by a significant predominance of firm mortality over births. Decision-makers abandon policies supporting the EE, redirecting their efforts toward other objectives, such as city promotion or increasing regional attractiveness (Mack & Mayer, 2016). Policy may thus return to its starting point, potentially seeding the emergence of a new EE. This suggests that EEs may fluctuate in a manner similar to macroeconomic business cycle phases. Currently, the literature lacks studies on the impact of evolutionary changes in EEs on SHG of firms. Evolutionary theories of EE development assume a certain developmental sequence – the current state of an EE largely depends on its condition in the previous period, and its evolution is based on adjustments to emerging disturbances (Kantis & Federico, 2020; Mack & Mayer, 2016; Thai et al., 2023). Similarly, EE actors evolve at different stages of ecosystem development.

These evolutionary processes can be enhanced and stimulated by policy arrangements, including the promotion of entrepreneurial achievements at different development stages. Events, such as awards for the best entrepreneur, play a significant role in promoting an entrepreneurial culture (Hermanto & Suryanto, 2017). Moreover, such competitions can be used to promote the concept of EEs, as success stories are often more persuasive than dry facts (Hermanto & Suryanto, 2017). This is particularly important in the early stages of EE development, because as the ecosystem grows, entrepreneurial activity increases, and individual actions attract less attention (Roundy & Bayer, 2019).

Policy evaluation for the upgrade of further directions and measures is often based on the comparative ranking and metrics of EEs. Various metrics have been developed to compare EEs, which are useful for assessing the effectiveness of implemented measures. Examples include the Global Entrepreneurship Monitor and the now-defunct Kaufmann Index (Spigel et al., 2020). Comparative assessment, however, is difficult, because even if a common method for EE evaluation is developed, the fragmentation of data complicates its application, especially in an international context.

A challenge in some countries is the lack of coordination between different levels of government, which can result in overlapping tasks. Understanding the configuration of the ecosystem allows local authorities to adapt policies to the specific characteristics of the EE (Gancarczyk, 2019). Since regions are not isolated entities, the economic situation in one region may affect neighboring EEs. In other words, there should be spillover effects between EEs. Therefore, EE policies should be coordinated with policymakers from neighboring regions.

Coordinating policies across neighboring ecosystems should enhance the first law of geography. Tobler's first law states that objects closer in space are more similar than those farther apart (Tobler, 2004). Consequently, adjacent EEs should generate similar outcomes, implying positive spatial autocorrelation. Negative spatial autocorrelation would indicate competition between EEs, while no correlation would suggest no spatial interaction and a random distribution of productive entrepreneurship levels.

Currently, few studies examine spatial interactions between EEs, particularly regarding the spatial interaction of EE outcomes, which constitutes a research gap worth addressing and leads to the formulation of Hypothesis 3.

H3. *The impact of entrepreneurial ecosystems on the productive growth of enterprises is moderated by spatial interactions between these ecosystems.*

Major cities functioning as administrative centers shape the framework for conducting business in the region. Therefore, any concept of EE development should also be coordinated with the authorities of the main urban centers in the region (Santinha et al., 2019). The character and distance of the influence of these major centers remains an under-researched area. EEs derive much of their strength from well-developed urban centers (Audretsch & Belitski, 2017). Consequently, heterogeneity in the impact of EEs is expected across areas with varying degrees of urbanization, and urbanization level can thus serve as a control variable in studies on the impact of EEs on productive enterprise growth.

Through proper interventions, it is possible to establish an EE from the grassroots. For example, the online gaming ecosystem in South Korea began forming in the early 1990s, and initially, the government was not supportive of the gaming industry. The development impetus came from high-speed internet infrastructure support around 1995 and the liberalization of telecommunications law in 1997. Both measures led to rapid industry growth, making it globally competitive. However, supporting specific industries can be perceived as discrimination by entrepreneurs in other industries.

In summary, EEs are a complex concept, and their implementation in economic policy must consider a range of national and regional conditions. This makes EE development policy challenging and necessitates research to guide it and support the selection of intervention tools.

Bibliography

Acs, Z. J., Autio, E., & Szerb, L. (2014). National systems of entrepreneurship: Measurement issues and policy implications. *Research Policy*, *43*(3), 476–494.

Acs, Z. J., Stam, E., Audretsch, D. B., & O'Connor, A. (2017). The lineages of the entrepreneurial ecosystem approach. *Small Business Economics*, *49*(1), 1–10. https://doi.org/10.1007/s11187-017-9864-8

Alam, A., Ghatak, A., & Bhowmick, B. (2023). Analysing the Influence of Components of Entrepreneurial Ecosystem on the Entrepreneurial Process. *ECIE 2023 18th European Conference on Innovation and Entrepreneurship Vol 1*. https://books.google.com/books?hl=en&lr=&id=3nrcEAAAQBAJ&oi=fnd&pg=PA8&dq=Analysing+the+Influence+of+Components+of+Entrepreneurial+Ecosystem+on+the+Entrepreneurial+Process&ots=bdJl4zoQCA&sig=gWqKAO4gYMMT7-7m-dC7sEhjO24

Alvedalen, J., & Boschma, R. (2017). A critical review of entrepreneurial ecosystems research: Towards a future research agenda. *European Planning Studies*, *25*(6), 887–903. https://doi.org/10.1080/09654313.2017.1299694

Audretsch, D. B., & Belitski, M. (2017). Entrepreneurial ecosystems in cities: Establishing the framework conditions. *The Journal of Technology Transfer*, *42*(5), 1030–1051. https://doi.org/10.1007/s10961-016-9473-8

Audretsch, D. B., Heger, D., & Veith, T. (2015). Infrastructure and entrepreneurship. *Small Business Economics*, *44*(2), 219–230. https://doi.org/10.1007/s11187-014-9600-6

Audretsch, D. B., & Link, A. N. (2019). Embracing an entrepreneurial ecosystem: An analysis of the governance of research joint ventures. *Small Business Economics*, *52*(2), 429–436. https://doi.org/10.1007/s11187-017-9953-8

Auerswald, P. E., & Dani, L. (2017). The adaptive life cycle of entrepreneurial ecosystems: The biotechnology cluster. *Small Business Economics*, *49*(1), 97–117. https://doi.org/10.1007/s11187-017-9869-3

Baker, T., & Welter, F. (2020). *Contextualizing entrepreneurship theory*. https://library.oapen.org/handle/20.500.12657/46740

Baumol, W. J. (1996). Entrepreneurship: Productive, unproductive, and destructive. *Journal of Business Venturing*, *11*(1), 3–22.

Baumol, W. J., Nelson, R. R., & Wolff, E. N. (1994). *Convergence of productivity: Cross-national studies and historical evidence*. Oxford University Press.

Blanka, C., & Traunmüller, V. (2020). Blind date? Intermediaries as matchmakers on the way to start-up—industry coopetition. *Industrial Marketing Management*, *90*, 1–13.

Brixiova, Z. (2010). Unlocking productive entrepreneurship in Africa's least developed countries*. *African Development Review*, *22*(3), 440–451. https://doi.org/10.1111/j.1467-8268.2010.00255.x

Brown, R., & Mawson, S. (2019). Entrepreneurial ecosystems and public policy in action: A critique of the latest industrial policy blockbuster. *Cambridge Journal of Regions, Economy and Society*, *12*(3), 347–368.

Brown, R., Mawson, S., & Mason, C. (2017). Myth-busting and entrepreneurship policy: The case of high growth firms. *Entrepreneurship & Regional Development*, *29*(5–6), 414–443. https://doi.org/10.1080/08985626.2017.1291762

Cattaruzzo, S., & Teruel, M. (2022). On the heterogeneity of the long-term leverage-growth relationship: A cross-country analysis of manufacturing firms. *Structural Change and Economic Dynamics*, *62*, 552–565. https://doi.org/10.1016/j.strueco.2022.06.011

Cho, D. S., Ryan, P., & Buciuni, G. (2022). Evolutionary entrepreneurial ecosystems: A research pathway. *Small Business Economics*, *58*(4), 1865–1883. https://doi.org/10.1007/s11187-021-00487-4

Clayton, P., Feldman, M., & Montmartin, B. (2023). Entrepreneurial finance and regional ecosystem emergence. *Small Business Economics*, *62*, 1–29. https://doi.org/10.1007/s11187-023-00827-6

Coad, A., & Srhoj, S. (2023). Entrepreneurial ecosystems and regional persistence of high growth firms: A 'broken clock'critique. *Research Policy*, *52*(6), 104762.

Cohen, B. (2006). Sustainable valley entrepreneurial ecosystems. *Business Strategy and the Environment*, *15*(1), 1–14. https://doi.org/10.1002/bse.428

Colombelli, A., Paolucci, E., & Ughetto, E. (2019). Hierarchical and relational governance and the life cycle of entrepreneurial ecosystems. *Small Business Economics*, *52*(2), 505–521. https://doi.org/10.1007/s11187-017-9957-4

Davari, A., & Najmabadi, A. D. (2018). Entrepreneurial ecosystem and performance in Iran. In N. Faghih & M. R. Zali (Eds.), *Entrepreneurship ecosystem in the Middle East and North Africa (MENA)* (pp. 265–282). Springer International Publishing. https://doi.org/10.1007/978-3-319-75913-5_8

Deyanova, K., Brehmer, N., Lapidus, A., Tiberius, V., & Walsh, S. (2022). Hatching start-ups for sustainable growth: A bibliometric review on business incubators. *Review of Managerial Science*, *16*(7), 2083–2109. https://doi.org/10.1007/s11846-022-00525-9

Dosi, G., Grazzi, M., Moschella, D., Pisano, G., & Tamagni, F. (2020). Long-term firm growth: An empirical analysis of US manufacturers 1959–2015. *Industrial and Corporate Change*, *29*(2), 309–332. https://doi.org/10.1093/icc/dtz044

Dreher, A., & Gassebner, M. (2013). Greasing the wheels? The impact of regulations and corruption on firm entry. *Public Choice*, *155*(3–4), 413–432. https://doi.org/10.1007/s11127-011-9871-2

Foss, N. J. (1996). Higher-order industrial capabilities and competitive advantage. *Journal of Industry Studies*, *3*(1), 1–20. https://doi.org/10.1080/13662719600000001

Foster, G., Shimizu, C., Ciesinski, S., Davila, A., Hassan, S., Jia, N., & Morris, R. (2013). Entrepreneurial ecosystems around the globe and company growth dynamics. *World Economic Forum*, *11*(2), 145–159.

Gancarczyk, M. (2019). The performance of high-growers and regional entrepreneurial ecosystems: A research framework. *Entrepreneurial Business and Economics Review*, *7*(3), 99–123. https://doi.org/10.15678/EBER.2019.070306

Gancarczyk, M., Gancarczyk, J., & Reichel, M. (Ed. Gancarczyk, M.) (2023). Revitalizing forgotten spaces through local leadership and social entrepreneurial ecosystems: The case of Muszyna commune. In *European Regional Policy and Development* (pp. 105–134). Routledge.

Gancarczyk, M., & Konopa, S. (2021). Exploring the governance of entrepreneurial ecosystems for productive high growth. *Foresight and STI Governance*, *15*(4), 9–21.

Gancarczyk, M., Tomczyk, D., & Gancarczyk, J. (2025). Sustainable industrial transformation through entrepreneurial ecosystem governance: The case of Polish energy clusters. *Entrepreneurial Business and Economics Review*, *13*(1), 95–118.

Gnyawali, D. R., & Fogel, D. S. (1994). Environments for entrepreneurship development: Key dimensions and research implications. *Entrepreneurship Theory and Practice*, *18*(4), 43–62. https://doi.org/10.1177/104225879401800403

Goetz, M. (2006). Atrakcyjność klastrów dla bezpośrednich inwestycji zagranicznych (BIZ). *International Journal of Management and Economics*, *20*. https://bazhum.muzhp.pl/media/files/International_Journal_of_Management_and_Economics/International_Journal_of_Management_and_Economics-r2006-t20/International_Journal_of_Management_and_Economics-r2006-t20-s8-23/International_Journal_of_Management_and_Economics-r2006-t20-s8-23.pdf

Hassna, G. (2022). Crowdfund smart, not hard–Understanding the role of online funding communities in crowdfunding success. *Journal of Business Venturing Insights, 18*, e00353.

Hermanto, B., & Suryanto, S. E. (2017). Entrepreneurship ecosystem policy in Indonesia. *Mediterranean Journal of Social Sciences, 8*(1). https://www.richtmann.org/journal/index.php/mjss/article/view/9668/9307

Hoang, H., & Antoncic, B. (2003). Network-based research in entrepreneurship: A critical review. *Journal of Business Venturing, 18*(2), 165–187.

Isenberg, D. (2011). *The Entrepreneurship Ecosystem Strategy as a New Paradigm for Economic Policy: Principles for Cultivating Entrepreneurship.*

Isenberg, D. J. (2010). How to start an entrepreneurial revolution. *Harvard Business Review, 88*(6), 40–50.

Johannisson, B., Alexanderson, O., Nowicki, K., & Senneseth, K. (1994). Beyond anarchy and organization: Entrepreneurs in contextual networks. *Entrepreneurship & Regional Development, 6*(4), 329–356. https://doi.org/10.1080/08985629400000020

Johannisson, B., & Mønsted, M. (1997). Contextualizing entrepreneurial networking: The case of scandinavia. *International Studies of Management & Organization, 27*(3), 109–136. https://doi.org/10.1080/00208825.1997.11656715

Kansheba, J. M. P. (2020). Small business and entrepreneurship in Africa: The nexus of entrepreneurial ecosystems and productive entrepreneurship. *Small Enterprise Research, 27*(2), 110–124. https://doi.org/10.1080/13215906.2020.1761869

Kantis, H., & Federico, J. (2020). A dynamic model of entrepreneurial ecosystems evolution. *Journal of Evolutionary Studies in Business, 5*(1), 182–220.

Koroleva, E. (2022). FinTech entrepreneurial ecosystems: Exploring the interplay between input and output. *International Journal of Financial Studies, 10*(4), 92.

Kreuzer, A., Mengede, K., Oppermann, A., & Regh, M. (2018). Guide for mapping the entrepreneurial ecosystem. *Deutsche Gesellschaft Für Internationale Zusammenarbeit: Bonn, Germany.*

Leendertse, J., Schrijvers, M., & Stam, E. (2022). Measure twice, cut once: Entrepreneurial ecosystem metrics. *Research Policy, 51*(9), 104336.

Liguori, E., Bendickson, J., Solomon, S., & McDowell, W. C. (2019). Development of a multi-dimensional measure for assessing entrepreneurial ecosystems. *Entrepreneurship & Regional Development, 31*(1–2), 7–21. https://doi.org/10.1080/08985626.2018.1537144

Lubis, A. S., Wijaya, C., & Sakapurnama, E. (2023). Analysis of entrepreneurial ecosystem factors on productive entrepreneurship of digital start-ups in Indonesia. *International Journal of Business Ecosystem & Strategy (2687–2293), 5*(3), 11–21.

Lucas, D. S., & Fuller, C. S. (2017). Entrepreneurship: Productive, unproductive, and destructive—Relative to what? *Journal of Business Venturing Insights, 7*, 45–49.

Mack, E., & Mayer, H. (2016). The evolutionary dynamics of entrepreneurial ecosystems. *Urban Studies, 53*(10), 2118–2133. https://doi.org/10.1177/0042098015586547

Mackiewicz, M., & Kurczewska, A. (2023). Is it the survival of the fittest or of the jacks-of-all-trades? Business survival in the light of Lazear's theory. *BRQ Business Research Quarterly, 26*(2), 167–180. https://doi.org/10.1177/2340944420976652

Mandrysz, W. (2020). Community-based social economy–social capital and civic participation in social entrepreneurship and community development. *Management Dynamics in the Knowledge Economy, 8*(1), 81–93.

Mason, C., & Brown, R. (2014). Entrepreneurial ecosystems and growth oriented entrepreneurship. *Final Report to OECD, Paris, 30*(1), 77–102.

Matt, M., & Schaeffer, V. (2018). Building entrepreneurial ecosystems conducive to student entrepreneurship: New challenges for universities. *Journal of Innovation Economics & Management*, *1*, 9–32.

McAdam, M., Harrison, R. T., & Leitch, C. M. (2019). Stories from the field: Women's networking as gender capital in entrepreneurial ecosystems. *Small Business Economics*, *53*(2), 459–474. https://doi.org/10.1007/s11187-018-9995-6

McKelvie, A., & Wiklund, J. (2010). Advancing firm growth research: A focus on growth mode instead of growth rate. *Entrepreneurship Theory and Practice*, *34*(2), 261–288.

Mohmand, Y. T., Mehmood, F., Mughal, K. S., & Aslam, F. (2021). Investigating the causal relationship between transport infrastructure, economic growth and transport emissions in Pakistan. *Research in Transportation Economics*, *88*, 100972.

Mungila Hillemane, B. S. (2020). Entrepreneurial ecosystem for tech start-ups in Bangalore: An exploration of structure and gap. *Journal of Small Business and Enterprise Development*, *27*(7), 1167–1185. https://doi.org/10.1108/JSBED-07-2019-0233

Neubaum, D. O., Kammerlander, N., & Brigham, K. H. (2019). Capturing family firm heterogeneity: How taxonomies and typologies can help the field move forward. *Family Business Review*, *32*(2), 106–130. https://doi.org/10.1177/0894486519848512

Nicotra, M., Romano, M., Del Giudice, M., & Schillaci, C. E. (2018). The causal relation between entrepreneurial ecosystem and productive entrepreneurship: A measurement framework. *The Journal of Technology Transfer*, *43*, 640–673.

Novela, S., Syarief, R., Fahmi, I., & Arkeman, Y. (2021). Creating a university-based entrepreneurial ecosystem in Indonesia. *Academic Journal of Interdisciplinary Studies*, *10*(1), 174–174.

Penrose, E. (1959). *Theory of the growth*. John Wiley & Sons.

Pietkun, P. (2024). *Samorządowe akty prawa miejscowego jako instrument służący wspieraniu lokalnej przedsiębiorczości–przykład uchwał w sprawie opłaty targowej*, University of Wrocław, 85–99.

Purbasari, R., Muttaqin, Z., & Sari, D. S. (2021). Digital entrepreneurship in pandemic Covid 19 era: The digital entrepreneurial ecosystem framework. *Review of Integrative Business and Economics Research*, *10*, 114–135.

Purbasari, R., Wijaya, C., & Rahayu, N. (2020). Most roles actors play in entrepreneurial ecosystem: A network theory perspective. *Journal of Entrepreneurship Education*, *23*(2), 1–16.

Qian, H. (2018). Knowledge-based regional economic development: A synthetic review of knowledge spillovers, entrepreneurship, and entrepreneurial ecosystems. *Economic Development Quarterly*, *32*(2), 163–176. https://doi.org/10.1177/0891242418760981

Qian, H., Acs, Z. J., & Stough, R. R. (2013). Regional systems of entrepreneurship: The nexus of human capital, knowledge and new firm formation. *Journal of Economic Geography*, *13*(4), 559–587.

Roundy, P. T. (2017). Social entrepreneurship and entrepreneurial ecosystems: Complementary or disjoint phenomena? *International Journal of Social Economics*, *44*(9), 1252–1267.

Roundy, P. T., & Bayer, M. A. (2019). Entrepreneurial ecosystem narratives and the micro-foundations of regional entrepreneurship. *The International Journal of Entrepreneurship and Innovation*, *20*(3), 194–208. https://doi.org/10.1177/1465750318808426

Roundy, P. T., Brockman, B. K., & Bradshaw, M. (2017). The resilience of entrepreneurial ecosystems. *Journal of Business Venturing Insights*, *8*, 99–104.

Roundy, P., & Evans, W. (2023). Entrepreneurial ecosystems as multiteam systems: Navigating independence and interdependence in the leadership of startup communities. *Journal of Business Venturing Insights*, *21*, e00445. https://doi.org/10.1016/j.jbvi.2023.e00445

Santinha, G., Dias, A., Rodrigues, M., Queirós, A., Rodrigues, C., Rocha, N.P. (2019). How Do Smart Cities Impact on Sustainable Urban Growth and on Opportunities for Entrepreneurship? Evidence from Portugal: The Case of Águeda. In: Cagica Carvalho, L., Rego, C., Lucas, M.R., Sánchez-Hernández, M.I., Backx Noronha Viana, A. (eds) New Paths of Entrepreneurship Development. Studies on Entrepreneurship, Structural Change and Industrial Dynamics. Springer, 31–53.

Schrijvers, M., Stam, E., & Bosma, N. (2024). Figuring it out: Configurations of high-performing entrepreneurial ecosystems in Europe. *Regional Studies*, *58*(5), 1096–1110. https://doi.org/10.1080/00343404.2023.2226727

Simón-Moya, V., Revuelto-Taboada, L., & Guerrero, R. F. (2014). Institutional and economic drivers of entrepreneurship: An international perspective. *Journal of Business Research*, *67*(5), 715–721.

Sobel, R. S. (2008). Testing Baumol: Institutional quality and the productivity of entrepreneurship. *Journal of Business Venturing*, *23*(6), 641–655.

Spigel, B. (2017). The relational organization of entrepreneurial ecosystems. *Entrepreneurship Theory and Practice*, *41*(1), 49–72. https://doi.org/10.1111/etap.12167

Spigel, B., Kitagawa, F., & Mason, C. (2020). A manifesto for researching entrepreneurial ecosystems. *Local Economy: The Journal of the Local Economy Policy Unit*, *35*(5), 482–495. https://doi.org/10.1177/0269094220959052

Stam, E., & Spigel, B. (2016). *Entrepreneurial ecosystems*. USE Discussion paper series. https://www.torrossa.com/gs/resourceProxy?an=5018791&publisher=FZ7200#page=436

Stam, E., & Van De Ven, A. (2021). Entrepreneurial ecosystem elements. *Small Business Economics*, *56*(2), 809–832. https://doi.org/10.1007/s11187-019-00270-6

Suresh, J., & Ramraj, R. (2012). Entrepreneurial ecosystem: Case study on the influence of environmental factors on entrepreneurial success. *European Journal of Business and Management*, *4*(16), 95–101.

Tapsi, S. A., & Baga, L. M. (2024). Role of entrepreneurial ecosystems to productive entrepreneurship. *IOP Conference Series: Earth and Environmental Science*, *1359*(1), 012046. https://iopscience.iop.org/article/10.1088/1755-1315/1359/1/012046/meta

Thai, Q. H., Mai, K. N., & Do, T. T. (2023). An evolution of entrepreneurial ecosystem studies: A systematic literature review and future research agenda. *Sage Open*, *13*(1), 21582440231153060. https://doi.org/10.1177/21582440231153060

Tlaiss, H. A., & McAdam, M. (2021). Unexpected lives: The intersection of Islam and Arab women's entrepreneurship. *Journal of Business Ethics*, *171*(2), 253–272. https://doi.org/10.1007/s10551-020-04437-0

Tobler, W. (2004). On the first law of geography: A reply. *Annals of the Association of American Geographers*, *94*(2), 304–310. https://doi.org/10.1111/j.1467-8306.2004.09402009.x

Torres, P., & Godinho, P. (2022). Levels of necessity of entrepreneurial ecosystems elements. *Small Business Economics*, *59*(1), 29–45. https://doi.org/10.1007/s11187-021-00515-3

Wurth, B., Stam, E., & Spigel, B. (2022). Toward an entrepreneurial ecosystem research program. *Entrepreneurship Theory and Practice*, *46*(3), 729–778. https://doi.org/10.1177/1042258721998948

Zbierowski, P. (2021). *Orientacja pozytywna organizacji wysokiej efektywności*. Wolters Kluwer Polska.

3 Empirical study methodology and characteristics of the research sample

3.1 Research model, methods, and procedure

The research problem addressed in the monograph concerns the impact of entrepreneurial ecosystems on the sustainable high growth of enterprises. Consequently, the main objective of the monograph, including the empirical study, is to determine the influence of EEs on the sustainable high growth of firms. The research model (Figure 3.1) assumes an effect on SHG as the dependent variable, coming from the EE as the main explanatory variable. The concept of SHG integrates the ideas of productive entrepreneurship and high-growth enterprises, thereby representing sustainable (long-term) high growth that features economic efficiency and social value in the form of employment growth. SHG is a theoretical variable, a complex construct represented by five observable variables: enterprise size growth, profitability, financial liquidity, solvency, and employment growth. Growth is measured by revenue dynamics, that is, the average annual increase in revenues over the past three years; profitability is expressed by ROE, financial liquidity by the current liquidity ratio, and solvency by the financial solvency ratio.

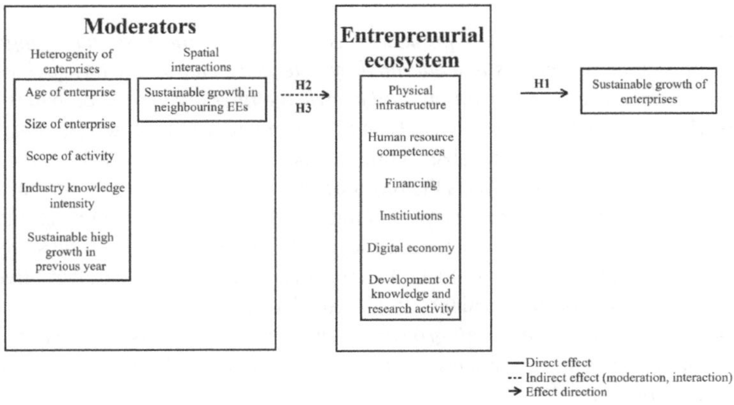

Figure 3.1 The research model

DOI: 10.4324/9781003739333-4

EE is a composite variable consisting of theoretically defined dimensions (components or elements), including the dimension of human resource competencies, institutions, financing, physical infrastructure, the digital economy, and the development of knowledge and research activity. EEs express the impact of the regional environment on SHG (H1).

The model also assumes the influence of resource-based factors related to firm heterogeneity as moderators of the impact of EE on SHG. Heterogeneity includes variations in firm characteristics such as age, size, scope of activity (diversification), knowledge intensity of the activity (H2.1), and previous SHG as a base for achieving SHG in a subsequent period (H2.2). A potential moderator of the EE– SHG relationship is also spatial interactions, that is, the mutual influence between geographically proximate EEs (H3).

The framework is based on the following research hypotheses:

H1. *Sustainable high growth of enterprises depends on the structural characteristics of entrepreneurial ecosystems.*

H1 reflects the assumption that EEs exert a differentiated impact on the sustainable high growth of enterprises, and this impact depends on the structural characteristics of the EE. In terms of structure, EEs are treated as combinations of dimensions expressed through synthetic variables.

H2. *The heterogeneity of enterprises operating within entrepreneurial ecosystems moderates the impact of these ecosystems on sustainable high growth of enterprises.*

H2 expresses the assumption that the moderating factor in the relationship between EE and SHG is the specificity and diversity of enterprises operating within the EE, defined as heterogeneity.

H2.1. *The influence of entrepreneurial ecosystems on the sustainable high growth of enterprises is moderated by enterprise characteristics such as age, size, scope of operations, and knowledge intensity of their activities.*

H2.1. holds that the influence of EE on SHG is moderated by enterprise characteristics such as age, size, scope of operations, and knowledge intensity. Heterogeneity reflects the resource-based view, which suggests that a firm's internal resources play a dominant role in its growth and its ability to leverage the environment to achieve SHG. In the case where the study finds no effect of EE on SHG, heterogeneity may provide an alternative explanation for the sustainable high growth of enterprises.

H2.2. *Prior sustainable high growth of enterprises moderates the impact of entrepreneurial ecosystems on future sustainable high growth of these enterprises.*

The evolutionary and resource-based approaches assume that earlier SHG generates SHG at a later time (Penrose, 1959). Hypothesis 2.2 posits that the prior ability to achieve profitable and sustainable growth moderates the influence of EE on SHG. If H1 is rejected, this capability may turn out to be a key determinant and the main independent variable (similar to other aspects of heterogeneity, i.e., the differentiated characteristics of enterprises mentioned in H2.1).

H3. *The impact of entrepreneurial ecosystems on the sustainable high growth of enterprises is moderated by spatial interactions between proximate ecosystems.*

H3. reflects the assumption of a positive spatial autocorrelation of SHG and a moderating effect of spatial interactions between EEs on SHG. If the influence of EP on SHG is rejected, this factor may serve as an alternative explanation of SHG, just like the resource-based factors.

The research procedure included the following steps:

- analysis of the literature;
- formulation of the research problem, the main objective, and specific objectives of the empirical study;
- formulation of research hypotheses resulting from the literature review;
- selection of the subject as well as the temporal and geographical scope of the study;
- determination of the indicator describing the sustainable high growth of enterprises;
- selection of research methods allowing for the verification of hypotheses;
- data processing;
- development and analysis of econometric models, evaluation of their quality, and interpretation of the obtained results.

The focus of the study is the relationship between SHG of enterprises and the EEs. The subject, geographical, and temporal scope of the study includes the structural characteristics of enterprises and regions (understood as Polish voivodeships) in the years 2018–2022. The focus on administrative units is justified both by the availability of statistical data and by the role of voivodeship authorities in shaping economic development policy. The role of regional authorities in shaping EEs allows for practical implications of the conclusions and recommendations resulting from the study. In this monograph, the EE will therefore be defined geographically by the administrative boundaries of the voivodeship.

The research methods included the narrative and critical literature review method in the theoretical part, and the secondary data analysis method for verifying research hypotheses in the empirical part. In implementing the secondary data analysis method, a set of research techniques was applied (Table 3.1). These included econometric techniques (panel logistic regression with random effects, Bayesian logistic regression), statistical techniques (Moran's I), and machine learning methods (spectral clustering analysis). Due to the origin of the data from various sources and their considerable volume (over 2 TB), big data processing techniques were also employed. These included text mining, web scraping, and techniques from Geographic Information Systems and geostatistics. Optimization techniques were used for data and model fitting.

3.2 Operationalization and measurement of variables; data sources

Table 3.2 presents the operationalization of the variables included in the research model (Figure 3.1). The variables are described in terms of their definitions, sources, and their relevance to the research hypotheses.

Table 3.3 presents the measurement of variables and data sources. The measurement process posed several challenges, including the need to develop a unique database compiled from diverse sources, with heterogeneous time ranges and data gaps. Taking into account the variability of time intervals and the availability of data with minimal missing values, the analysis focused on the period 2018–2022. This timeframe includes the COVID-19 pandemic; however, due to the lack of financial data prior to 2018, it was not possible to conduct a reliable analysis for earlier years.

Given the highly stochastic nature of the dependent variable, it was not feasible to conduct a formal test for structural changes. Nevertheless, a visual analysis of the share of productive-growth enterprises across regions in different years did not reveal structural changes in 2020, which was the first year potentially affected by the COVID-19 pandemic. At the same time, the share of high-growth enterprises – the basis for identifying productive-growth enterprises – ranged from 2.5% to 6% across voivodeships, which aligns with most previous studies. Visual inspection of regional data also did not indicate the presence of structural changes.

Construction of the synthetic indicator of sustainable high growth

A company is classified as belonging to the group of SHG enterprises if it has recorded an average annual employment growth of at least 20% over the past three years. In addition, the average combined percentile of the following four indicators must be at least 75%:

- Return on Equity (ROE);
- Solvency ratio;
- Financial liquidity ratio;
- Employment growth rate.

Table 3.1 Techniques used in the study and the purpose of their application

Group of employed techniques	*Use tool*	*Purpose of application*
Econometric techniques	Panel logistic regression with random effects	Verification of H1, H2, and H3
	Marginal effects	Verification of H2 and H3
	Bayesian logistic regression	Auxiliary use: evaluation of regression parameter behavior
	Linear regression	Auxiliary use: assessment of the impact of entrepreneurial ecosystems on the share of high-growth enterprises in entrepreneurial ecosystems, for comparison with other studies
Machine learning techniques	Spectral clustering analysis	Verification of H1
Statistical techniques	Moran's I statistic	Verification of H3
	Directional local indicator of spatial association (directional LISA)	Auxiliary use: evaluation of spatial interactions changes over time
	Nonlinear correlation coefficient ξ	Auxiliary use: assessment of nonlinearity of changes after weighting
Big data processing techniques	Text mining	Auxiliary use: processing data from Central Registration and Information on Business (CEIDG) and National Court Register (KRS); processing data from registers maintained by the Polish Financial Supervision Authority (KNF)
	Webscrapping	Auxiliary use: data collection from registers maintained by the Polish Financial Supervision Authority
	Geographic Information Systems (GIS) and geostatistical methods	Auxiliary use: geolocation of enterprises based on address; aggregation of enterprises, bank branches, and data from the Topographic Objects Database in individual entrepreneurial ecosystems; buffer analysis to calculate the local urbanization index; coordinate system conversion of spatial data from various sources
Optimization techniques	Variable weighting	Adjustment of the structure of EE dimensions to the data and model in order to optimally fit the panel logistic regression model

Source: Own elaboration.

Table 3.2 Operationalization of variables

Variable in the model	*Variable description*	*Source*	*Link to hypotheses*
Dependent variable			
Sustainable high growth of enterprises (dependent variable)	A concept that combines the idea of productive entrepreneurship with the notion of high-growth firms; a variable linking rapid revenue growth with sustainability – that is, profitability, solvency, and financial liquidity – as well as employment growth as a social value.	Baumol (1996); Gancarczyk and Konopa (2021); Mason and Brown (2010)	**H1.** Sustainable high growth of enterprises depends on the structural characteristics of entrepreneurial ecosystems.
Independent variables – dimensions of EE			
Dimension of physical infrastructure	Physical infrastructure, understood as the combination of transport infrastructure and real estate designated for business activity, supports exchange within entrepreneurial ecosystems as well as on national and international scales, and stimulates both local and foreign investments.	Charles and Zegarra (2014); Krugman (1991); Penrose (1959); Stam and Van De Ven (2021); Torres and Godinho (2022); Williamson (1971, p. 971)	**H1.** Sustainable high growth of enterprises depends on the structural characteristics of entrepreneurial ecosystems.
Dimension of human resource competence	The level of education in society influences the location of knowledge-intensive business activities. The share of doctoral students and participants in lifelong learning within the population fosters the development and updating of competencies and the implementation of innovations.	Charles and Zegarra (2014); Gancarczyk and Konopa (2021); Isenberg (2011); Liguori et al. (2019); Penrose (1959); Torres and Godinho (2022)	**H1.** Sustainable high growth of enterprises depends on the structural characteristics of entrepreneurial ecosystems.

Dimension of access to finance	Access to credit and loans enables investments and high enterprise growth. The number and diversity of financial institutions affect the ability to choose efficient forms of financing.	Isenberg (2011); Liguori et al. (2019); Suresh and Ramraj (2012); Torres and Godinho (2022)	**H1.** Sustainable high growth of enterprises depends on the structural characteristics of entrepreneurial ecosystems.
Dimension of institutional quality	Formal and informal rules, principles, and norms regulate the socio-economic environment and influence efficiency. High social capital and a cooperative mindset support economic exchange and collaboration among enterprises. The presence of business organizations and NGOs stimulates relationship building and network expansion. Low crime rates indicate environmental stability.	Foster et al. (2013); Gancarczyk and Konopa (2021); Isenberg (2011); Liguori et al. (2019); Putnam (1995); Stam and Van De Ven (2021)	**H1.** Sustainable high growth of enterprises depends on the structural characteristics of entrepreneurial ecosystems.
Dimension of the digital economy	Information and communication technologies reduce transaction costs and stimulate innovation, which serves as a foundation for enterprise growth.	Bejjani et al. (2023); Bouncken and Kraus (2022); Elia et al. (2020)	**H1.** Sustainable high growth of enterprises depends on the structural characteristics of entrepreneurial ecosystems.
Dimension of knowledge development and research activity	The development of knowledge and research activity can become a source of revenue growth and help reduce costs.	Gancarczyk and Konopa (2021); Gomes et al. (2023)	**H1.** Sustainable high growth of enterprises depends on the structural characteristics of entrepreneurial ecosystems.

(Continued)

Table 3.2 (Continued)

Variable in the model	*Variable description*	*Source*	*Link to hypotheses*
Moderators			
Age of the enterprise	Enterprise growth depends on its development stage and age.	Nelson et al. (2020); Nelson and Winter (1973); Penrose (1959)	**H2.** Heterogeneity of enterprises operating within entrepreneurial ecosystems moderates the impact of these ecosystems on productive enterprise growth.
Size of the enterprise	Enterprise growth depends on its size; the smaller the enterprise is, the higher is the probability of growth. Enterprises of different sizes have varying needs within entrepreneurial ecosystems.	Gancarczyk (2017); Penrose (1959)	**H2.** The influence of entrepreneurial ecosystems on the sustainable high growth of firms is moderated by the heterogeneity of the companies operating within these ecosystems.
Scope of activity	The ability to grow rapidly depends on the capability to leverage economies of scale and scope.	Panzar and Willig, (1981); Teece (1980, 1997)	**H2.** The influence of entrepreneurial ecosystems on the sustainable high growth of firms is moderated by the heterogeneity of the companies operating within these ecosystems.
Industry knowledge intensity	Enterprises engaged in knowledge-intensive activities demonstrate faster growth, as such activities are associated with higher innovativeness compared to those with lower knowledge intensity.	Penrose (1959)	**H2.** The influence of entrepreneurial ecosystems on the sustainable high growth of firms is moderated by the heterogeneity of the companies operating within these ecosystems.

Prior sustainable high growth	Enterprises that experienced prior sustainable high growth can accumulate resources for continued sustainable high growth.	Nelson and Winter (1973)	**H2.** The influence of entrepreneurial ecosystems on the sustainable high growth of firms is moderated by the heterogeneity of the companies operating within these ecosystems.
Sustainable high growth in neighboring entrepreneurial ecosystems	Geographic proximity leads to isomorphism (similarity of entities), promotes spatial interactions between EEs, and supports knowledge spillovers and economic development.	Anselin and Li (2020); Krugman (1991); Miller (2004); Sui (2004)	**H3.** The impact of entrepreneurial ecosystems on the sustainable high growth of enterprises is moderated by spatial interactions between proximate ecosystems.
Control variables			
Urbanization	-	Hartman and Kear (2024); Mitra et al. (2023)	-
Gross domestic product per capita for EE	-	Ashraf and Singh (2019); Singh et al. (2023)	-

Source: Own elaboration.

Table 3.3 Measurement of variables and data sources

Variable	*Variable description*	*Data source**	*Time scope used in the analysis***
Dependent variable			
Sustainable high growth of enterprises (*SHG*)	Synthetic artificial variable including: 1 Enterprise revenue dynamics (percentage increase compared to the previous year, accumulated over the last three years); 2 Return on equity ratio; 3 Financial liquidity ratio; 4 Solvency ratio; 5 Employment growth rate.	Data sources: Orbis (1) (2) (3) (4) (5);	2018–2022
Independent variables – dimensions of EE			
Dimension of physical infrastructure (*infr*)	Synthetic artificial variable including: 1 Road length in relation to the area of the EE; 2 Commercial and service building area in relation to the area of the EE; 3 Industrial and warehouse building area in relation to the area of the EE; 4 Length of telecommunication lines in relation to the area of the EE; 5 Air traffic volume (passengers) in relation to the area of the EE.	Local Data Bank (1) (5); Topographic Object Database 10k (2) (3) (4);	2018–2022
Dimension of human resource competence (*hc*)	Synthetic artificial variable including: 1 Number of PhD students relative to the population of EE; 2 Number of people who completed a language, computer, or practical skills course relative to the EE population; 3 High school graduation (matura exam) pass rate; 4 Percentage of people aged 15–64 with higher education.	Local Data Bank (1) (2) (3) (4);	2018–2022

(*Continued*)

Table 3.3 (Continued)

Variable	*Variable description*	*Data source**	*Time scope used in the analysis***
Dimension of financing (*fin*)	Synthetic artificial variable including: 1 Number of business angels relative to the number of enterprises in EE; 2 Number of venture capital funds relative to the number of enterprises in EE; 3 Number of business accelerators relative to the number of enterprises in EE; 4 Number of loan institutions relative to the number of enterprises in EE; 5 Number of bank branches relative to the number of enterprises in EE.	Crunchbase (1) (2) (3); Register of Loan Institutions maintained by the Polish Financial Supervision Authority (KNF) (4); OpenStreetMap (5);	2024
Dimension of institutions (*inst*)	Synthetic artificial variable including: 1 Number of reported crimes relative to the population EE; 2 Number of cultural centers, community centers, clubs, and cultural facilities relative to EE population; 3 Total number of memberships in non-profit organizations relative to EE population; 4 Share of innovative enterprises with more than nine employees that collaborate within a cluster initiative or another formalized network.	https://dane.gov.pl (1); Local Data Bank (2) (3) (4);	2018–2022 (1) (2) (4); 2018, 2020, 2022 (3)

(*Continued*)

Table 3.3 (Continued)

Variable	*Variable description*	*Data source**	*Time scope used in the analysis***
Dimension of the digital economy (*digi*)	Synthetic artificial variable including: 1 Share of small, medium, and large non-financial enterprises employing ICT specialists; 2 Share of enterprises with fixed broadband connections of at least 30Mb/s.	Local Data Bank (1) (2);	2018–2020; 2022 (1); 2018–2022 (2)
Dimension of knowledge development and research activity (*rd*)	Synthetic artificial variable including: 1 Total internal R&D expenditure relative to the number of enterprises; 2 Share of industrial enterprises that cooperated on innovation activities; 3 Share of service enterprises that cooperated on innovation activities; 4 Number of internal R&D personnel relative to EE population.	Local Data Bank (1) (2) (3) (4);	2018–2022
Moderators			
Age of the enterprise (age)	Variable describing enterprise heterogeneity. Its value reflects the number of years since the declared year of establishment.	National Court Register (via Statistics Poland API); Central Registration and Information on Business (via Statistics Poland API);	n/d
Size of the enterprise (size)	Value of enterprise assets.	Orbis;	2018–2022
Scope of activity (scope)	Variable describing enterprise heterogeneity. The range is expressed as the number of declared Polish Classification of Activities (PKD) codes in CEIDG or KRS.	National Court Register (Statistics Poland API, JSON format); Central Registration and Information on Business (Statistics Poland API, JSON format);	2024

(*Continued*)

Table 3.3 (Continued)

Variable	*Variable description*	*Data source**	*Time scope used in the analysis***
Industry knowledge intensity (know)	Synthetic variable describing enterprise heterogeneity, based on the number of PKD codes classified as knowledge-intensive industries (classified according to the Polish Classification of Activities and the NACE Rev.2 sector classification).	National Court Register (Statistics Poland API, JSON format); Central Registration and Information on Business (Statistics Poland API, JSON format); Eurostat;	2024
Prior sustainable high growth in the previous year (SHGt1)	Synthetic variable taking the value 1 if the enterprise recorded sustainable high growth in the previous period, and 0 otherwise.	Own calculations based on SHG;	2019–2022
Sustainable high growth in neighboring entrepreneurial ecosystems (SHGin)	Synthetic variable describing the average share of sustainable high-growth enterprises in neighboring EEs (sharing a border).	Own calculations based on SHG;	2018–2022
Control variables			
Urbanization (*urb*)	Percentage of built-up areas within a 1-km radius around each enterprise's location, based on OpenStreetMap.	Own calculations based on SHG; CORINE Land Cover 2018 (100 m raster map based on satellite data) (1); State Border Register (2); OpenStreetMap (3);	2018 (1);2024 (1) (3);
Gross domestic product per capita for EE (*gdpee*)	Gross domestic product per capita at the voivodeship level.	Local Data Bank	2018–2022

Source: Own elaboration.

* Numbers in parentheses indicate the variable number listed in the "Variable description" column.

** Numbers in parentheses also indicate the variable number listed in the "Data source" column.

The indicators included in the **top 25% criterion** have been defined as follows:

$$\text{ROE} = \frac{\text{net income}}{\text{average shareholders' equity}} \times 100\% \tag{3.1}$$

$$\text{Solvency ratio} = \frac{\text{total debt}}{\text{total assets}} \tag{3.2}$$

$$\text{Financial liquidity ratio} = \frac{\text{current assets}}{\text{current liabilities}} \tag{3.3}$$

$$\text{Employment growth rate} = \frac{\text{number of employees in the current year}}{\text{number of employees in the previous year}} \tag{3.4}$$

Construction of synthetic indicators of entrepreneurial ecosystems

Each variable included in the synthetic indicators of the ecosystem dimensions was defined as either a stimulant or a destimulant. The only destimulant is the number of crimes detected relative to the EE population. All other variables were treated as stimulants. Subsequently, quasi-optimal weights within each ecosystem dimension were determined. The technical aspects of constructing the synthetic indicators for the dimensions of the EE are discussed later in this chapter. In addition to the synthetic indicators for individual dimensions, a synthetic indicator of the aggregated EE (agr_ee) was constructed. This indicator is a standardized sum of the synthetic indicators of the six ecosystem dimensions. Its values generally fall within the range from -4 to 4, where a higher value indicates a more developed ecosystem.

3.3 Characteristics of data sources and the data collection and processing procedure

Characteristics of databases used in the study

The Orbis database provided by Moody's Analytics was used as the source of financial data on enterprises. This database includes, among other things, raw and processed address and financial data, indicators evaluating business entities, and media mentions related to them. The construction of the database relies on data from 133 information providers, including the Polish-registered company InfoCredit. The following procedure was applied to extract the final research sample (the first number in parentheses indicates the number of enterprises, the second – the number of observations):

- Entities in Poland for which data were available in the Orbis database were identified (3,201,350);
- Entities lacking sales data for seven consecutive years were filtered out (76,145);

- A random sample of 70,000 entities was drawn from the above group (limited by the data download cap from Orbis) (70,000; 350,000);
- Observations lacking data on total assets were removed (69,751; 348,875);
- Observations for the years 2023 and 2017 or earlier were removed (69,751; 342,340);
- Only limited liability companies, joint-stock companies, registered partnerships, capital companies, civil law partnerships, European companies, capital-joint stock companies, state-owned enterprises, simple joint-stock companies, and sole proprietorships registered in CEIDG were included (61,003; 299,076);
- Observations with missing ROE data were filtered out (57,683; 268,891);
- Observations with missing solvency ratio data were filtered out (57,683; 268,649);
- Observations with missing liquidity ratio data were filtered out (52,936; 238,497);
- Observations with missing employment data were filtered out (45,173; 183,993);
- Enterprises for which it was not possible to obtain geographic coordinates or confirm their accuracy were filtered out (43,714; 178,163).

Data from *the National Court Register and the Central Registration and Information on Business Activity* are provided by Statistics Poland through the "REGON Internet Database 1" (BIR1) API, which allows for searching publicly available data based on NIP, KRS, and REGON numbers.

For each REGON number, two queries were made to both CEIDG and KRS.

- The first query retrieved basic information about registered companies;
- The second query allowed for downloading data on PKD codes.

The result of each query was a JSON (JavaScript Object Notation) file. To extract the required information, a traditional text mining method was used, specifically regular expression (regex) searching. Company geolocation was performed using the tidygeocoder package available in R. Two queries were made for each entity:

- The first query used the syntax: "full company name" + "voivodeship" + "locality" + "postal code";
- The second query used: "full company name" + "voivodeship" + "locality" + "building number."

The results from both procedures were merged into a single dataset. The coordinates assigned by OpenStreetMap were then validated for geographical correctness. It was verified whether the coordinates fell within the boundaries of the voivodeship, based on the State Register of Borders, in which the company was expected to be located according to GUS registers (KRS, CEIDG). Companies with incorrectly assigned coordinates were excluded from further analysis (see data processing in Orbis, point 11).

To calculate the local urbanization index, *the Corine Land Cover 2018 map* was used, available on request via the Copernicus service. This map is created as part of the Copernicus Programme, which is a component of the European Union Space Programme, and is updated on a six-year cycle. The map is based on satellite imagery from Sentinel, and in the version used in this study, the images covered the period 2017–2018. Based on these images, 44 land use classes were distinguished. The version used was the 2020_20u1 GeoTIFF map from the year 2020. The original map used EPSG:3035 coordinate format, which was transformed into WGS-84 for the purposes of this study. Around each pair of coordinates obtained via the OpenStreetMap API, three circular buffers were created with radii of 500 m, 1 km, and 2 km. For each circle, the share of pixels coded as 1 was calculated in relation to the total number of pixels within the shape. A visual inspection showed the best fit for the 1 km radius circle, which was further confirmed by statistical regression analysis.

Most of the regional data were downloaded in CSV format from *the Local Data Bank provided by the Statistics Poland.* Missing values were filled in using the arithmetic mean of the previous and following years. If the missing data concerned the first or last year of the series, data from the immediately preceding or following period were used, respectively. Missing data can be identified in Table 3.3, in the column titled *Time scope used in the analysis.* In the case of sustainable high growth in the previous period, due to a lack of available data, it was assumed to be absent for all enterprises. As a result, the impact of previous-period sustainable high growth on current SHG is likely underestimated. However, including data for the year 2018 helps to compensate for this limitation, contributing tens of thousands of observations that improve the precision of the estimation of other structural parameters in the model.

Data related to the financial dimension of the entrepreneurial ecosystem

Financial data on business angels, accelerators, and venture capital entities were obtained separately from the Crunchbase database, counted, and assigned to specific EE using regular expressions. Data on lending institutions were collected via web scraping from the Register of Credit Intermediaries and Lending Institutions, maintained by the Polish Financial Supervision Authority. Since the register contains information only at the locality (town/city) level, voivodeships were assigned using queries through BIR1, and the number of institutions in each region was then counted. Data on bank branches were downloaded from OpenStreetMap using the API available at https://overpass-turbo.eu/ and exported in GeoJSON format using the WGS-84 coordinate system. With the use of the National Register of Boundaries map, provided by the Head Office of Geodesy and Cartography, in a shapefile (SHP) format using the EPSG:2180 coordinate system, bank branches were aggregated for each voivodeship.

The Topographic Object Database (BDOT 10k) is a vector database with a level of detail corresponding to a 1:10,000 scale topographic map. BDOT 10k is made available through the portal https://www.geoportal.gov.pl. Data can be downloaded individually for each county and year, as the portal does not allow bulk downloading. Due to the regular structure of the download link format – which includes voivodeship and county codes – an R script was written to automatically retrieve all available data. The structure of the voivodeship and county codes was obtained from the website of the Association of Polish Counties (https://www.zpp.pl). The data were downloaded in the SHP format using the EPSG:2180 coordinate system. Information in BDOT 10k regarding commercial and industrial complexes was derived from orthophotos and manually verified in the field.

3.4 Research techniques employed

A variety of research techniques were applied to verify the research hypotheses and conduct supplementary analyses. This subsection provides a technical description of these methods.

Synthetic variables and weights

Formula for a stimulant:

$$S_i = \frac{X_i - X_{i_{\min}}}{X_{i_{\max}} - X_{i_{\min}}} \tag{3.5}$$

Formula for a destimulant:

$$S_i = \frac{X_{i_{\max}} - X_i}{X_{i_{\max}} - X_{i_{\min}}} \tag{3.6}$$

X_i – value of the variable for observation *i;*
$X_{i\max}$ – maximum value of the variable;
$X_{i\min}$ – minimum value of the variable;
S_i – synthetic indicator for observation *i*.

Within each dimension of the EE, quasi-optimal weights were determined using the Monte Carlo method. This procedure was carried out to better align the structure of variables with the data and the model. As a result, the variables whose levels and changes over time more accurately reflect the probability of achieving sustainable high growth were emphasized. At the same time, to avoid overfitting the model, the variables for each dimension were measured separately. The weights were chosen in such a way as to minimize the Akaike Information Criterion (AIC) of the panel logistic regression model.

$$y_{it} = \alpha_i + \beta x_{it} + \phi \chi_{it}^{\omega} + u_{it}, \quad i = 1,\ldots,N; t = 1,\ldots,T \tag{3.7}$$

$$\underset{\omega_1, \omega_2, \ldots, \omega_n}{\min} \Rightarrow AIC \tag{3.8}$$

The weights were drawn from a uniform distribution in the range [0;1], and their sum equals 1 for each dimension.

$$\omega_i \sim U[0;1]. \tag{3.9}$$

$$\sum_{i=1}^{n} \omega_i = 1 \tag{3.10}$$

Where:

y_{it} – observed artificial outcome variable;
a_i – unit-specific effect that is time-invariant;
x_{it} – vector of exogenous variables at time t (including the constant);
X_{it} – vector of exogenous variables at time t (subject to weighting);
P – vector of unknown regression coefficients;
ϕ – vector of unknown regression coefficients of variables with estimated weights;
ω – vector of weights;
u_{it} – residuals uncorrelated with the unit and over time;

The independent variables included in the regression (denoted by X) were know, size, numer_of_employees, urb, SHGin, and scope.

For each dimension, 1500 such regressions were calculated, and to determine the final weights, 15 random draws (1%) with the lowest AIC values were selected. The weights from these draws were averaged and applied in constructing the synthetic indicators of each dimension.

For the purpose of weighting, the variables were transformed using the following formula:

$$S_{n_i} = 1 - S_i \tag{3.11}$$

Where:

S_{ni} – stimulant/destimulant i at the time of weighting;

After weighting, the values of stimulants and destimulants were subtracted from 1, so that higher values indicated better performance, and standardization was applied using the following formula:

$$z = \frac{S_i - M(S_i)}{\sigma(S_i)} \tag{3.12}$$

Where:

$\mu(S_i)$ – arithmetic mean of stimulant/destimulant *i;*
$\sigma(S_i)$ – standard deviation of stimulant/destimulant *i*.

The weighting was performed twice. The first time, it was used to eliminate highly correlated variables ($|R| > 0.75$). In such cases, the variable with the highest weight was retained, and the remaining variables were removed from further analysis. Then, weighting was performed again to determine the final weights for the selected variables.

Panel logistic regression

The main research model used in the study is panel logistic regression with random effects, as it is not possible to estimate regression with fixed effects for the studied models. This method allows for the assessment of the impact of independent variables x_i on the probability that the dependent variable y_{it} belongs to one of two categories. The value 1 assigned to the artificial outcome variable corresponds to enterprises that recorded SHG, while the value 0 refers to the remaining enterprises. The application of the panel version of the regression enables consideration of unit effects during model estimation, thereby allowing for a more accurate estimation of the model's structural parameters.

Panel logistic regression can be described starting from the model:

$$y_{it} = \alpha_i + \beta x_{it} + u_{it}, \quad i = 1, \ldots, N; t = 1, \ldots, T \tag{3.13}$$

where:

y_{it} – observed artificial outcome variable;
a_j – unit-specific effect constant over time;
X_{it} – vector of exogenous variables at time *t* (including the constant term);
β – vector of unknown regression coefficients;
ε_{it} – error terms uncorrelated across units and time.

Assuming that the error terms follow a logistic distribution:

$$F(u) = \frac{1}{1 + e^{-u}}. \tag{3.14}$$

The probability of unit i belonging to a specific class at time t is:

$$\Pr\left(y_{it} = 1 \mid x_{it}, \alpha_i\right) = \frac{e^{\beta x_{it} + \alpha_i}}{1 + e^{\beta x_{it} + \alpha_i}} \tag{3.15}$$

$$\Pr\left(y_{it} = 0 \mid x_{it}, \alpha_i\right) = \frac{1}{1 + e\left(\alpha_i + \beta x_{it}\right)} \tag{3.16}$$

The individual effects are drawn from a normal distribution with a mean of 0 and variance σ_α^2.

$$\alpha_i \sim N\left(0, \sigma_\alpha^2\right) \tag{3.17}$$

The above model will be used to test all three hypotheses: H1, H2, and H3.

In particular, the vector x_{it} will include the following variables:

For H1

x_{it} denotes the vector of independent variables describing EEs, firms, clusters, and control variables for each unit *i* at time *t*.

For H2 and H3

x_{it} denotes the vector of independent variables describing entrepreneurial ecosystems, firms, clusters, the currently examined interaction, and control variables for each unit *i* at time *t*.

A backward stepwise regression will be used to select the final variables included in the models.

Moran's I statistic

Additionally, as part of the in-depth analysis of H3 regarding positive spatial autocorrelation, the global Moran's I statistic was used (Chen, 2013). It takes values in the range from –1 to 1. Values close to –1 indicate a spatial pattern where each spatial unit borders units that are maximally dissimilar. Values close to 0 suggest a spatial pattern resembling a random distribution. Values close to 1 indicate adjacency of units with similar values, that is, high spatial clustering.

$$I = \frac{N}{W} \frac{\sum_{i=1}^{N} \sum_{j=1}^{N} w_{ij} \left(x_i - \bar{x}\right)\left(x_j - \bar{x}\right)}{\sum_{i=1}^{N} \left(x_i - \bar{x}\right)^2} \tag{3.18}$$

Where:

N – number of spatial units indexed by variables i and j;
x – the variable under study;
$\bar{x}$ – mean of x;
w_{ij} – elements of the spatial weight matrix with zeros on the diagonal,
W – the sum of all w_{ij},

$$W = \sum_{i=1}^{N} \sum_{j=1}^{N} w_{ij} \tag{3.19}$$

The spatial weight was defined as 1 for EE sharing a common border, and 0 for all others.

The variable under analysis is the average share of PGE in a given EP over the years 2018–2022.

Directional local spatial association indicator

The directional local spatial association indicator (directional LISA), introduced by an extension of the LISA indicator originally proposed by L. Anselin in 1995 (Anselin, 1995), was calculated as a supporting metric in the in-depth analysis of the issue.

LISA at location i and time t is expressed by the formula:

$$L_{i,t} = \frac{z_{i,t} \sum_j w_{i,j} z_{j,t}}{\sum_i z_{i,t}^2} \tag{3.20}$$

Where:

z_{it} – the share of SHG enterprises in EE i at time t (expressed as a deviation from the mean),
w_{ij} – spatial weight defining neighborhood.

The LISA indicators were calculated for the years 2019–2020 and 2021–2022, followed by the generation of a standard Moran scatter plot and plots of differences (both non-standardized and standardized) between the two sets of LISA results.

$$s\left(x_i; x_j\right) = e^{\frac{-\|x_i - x_j\|^2}{2\sigma^2}} \tag{3.21}$$

and the graph Laplacian was calculated:

$$L = D - W \tag{3.22}$$

where:

L – graph Laplacian;
D – degree matrix of the graph;
W – similarity matrix of the graph.

Next, the eigenvalues of the Laplacian were calculated, and a matrix was constructed, whose eigenvectors became its columns. Subsequently, k-means clustering was performed using Euclidean distance as the metric.

Nonlinear correlation coefficient ξ

To assess nonlinear collinearity, the nonlinear correlation coefficient ξ was used.

$$\xi_n(X,Y) := 1 - \frac{n\sum_{i=1}^{n-1} \left| r_{i+1} = r_i \right|}{2\sum_{i=1}^{n} l_i\left(n - l_i\right)} \tag{3.23}$$

This requires a data transformation such that the following condition is met:

$$\left(X_{(1)}, Y_{(1)}\right), \ldots, \left(X_{(n)}, Y_{(n)}\right) \rightarrow X_{(1)} \leq \ldots X_{(n)}$$

Where:

X, Y – random variables,
n – number of observations;
r_i – rank of variable Y_i, number of observations such that $Y_i \geq Y_j$;
l_i – number of observations.

Marginal effects

To examine the moderating effects of resource variables and spatial interactions, panel logistic regressions with random effects were conducted, including an interaction term between the variables under study. For these models, marginal effects were also calculated using the formula from Bland and Cook (2019):

$$\text{ME}\left(X_i\right) = \frac{\delta Y}{\delta X_i} \tag{3.24}$$

Where ME(X_i) denotes the marginal effects of variable X_i, and $\partial Y/\partial X_i$ represents the derivative of variable Y with respect to X_i (a function representing the probability of an event). Marginal effects indicate how the outcome changes within a given space of other variables due to the change of a single variable, assuming the other variables remain constant. Since, in logistic regression, the impact of a variable's change depends on the values of other variables, the regression coefficients cannot be interpreted in terms of statistical significance (Greene, 2010). Marginal effects indicate the sign and direction of the change in probability, while the probability values themselves are not directly interpretable in logistic regression.

Using the panel structure of the data and the possibility that a firm may gain or lose the status of a sustainable high-growth enterprise, this effect was calculated based on status change dynamics, not cross-sectional comparison (as in the case of the variable SHGt1).

Linear regression

As a supplementary method to estimate the influence of the EE on the share of SHGE enterprises, a linear regression was computed:

$$y = \alpha + \beta x_i + \varepsilon_i \tag{3.25}$$

Where:

y – average share of PW enterprises in the years 2018–2022;
β – vector of unknown regression parameters;
x_i – average aggregated EP indicator in 2018–2022 for observation i;

Logistic regression

Additionally, for a more in-depth analysis, a Bayesian logistic regression was estimated, in which parameters were sampled using the standard Metropolis–Hastings algorithm.

The Bayesian panel regression was not used due to the long expected estimation time and licensing restrictions of the Stata SE version, which does not allow estimation of such a model on large samples.

$$y_{it} = \alpha_i + \beta x_i + u_i, \quad i = 1, \ldots, N; \tag{3.26}$$

y_{it} – observed artificial outcome variable;
α_i – intercept;
x_{it} – vector of exogenous variables at time t (including the intercept);
β – vector of unknown regression coefficients;
u_i – residuals uncorrelated across units and time;

The Metropolis–Hastings algorithm was run 20,000 times, with the first 10,000 draws discarded. Additionally, to reduce autocorrelation, every 10th draw was discarded (thinning). The prior distribution of the parameters was set using Stata's default settings: ~N(0, 10,000).

3.5 Characteristics of the research sample

General sample characteristics

Table 3.4 presents the characteristics of the enterprises in the sample by size class.

Table 3.4 shows that the research sample accurately reflects the ratio of medium-sized to large firms in the population of Polish enterprises (3.33 in the sample vs. 3.94 in the population). The ratio of small to medium-sized firms is represented less accurately (1.84 in the sample vs. 3.38 in the population), and there is a significant discrepancy in the ratio of micro to small firms (0.74 in the sample vs. 44.31 in the population). Despite these differences – which result from the nature of data available in the Orbis database – the structure

Table 3.4 Characteristics of the research sample and population by enterprise size class

Enterprise size class (number of employees)	*Number of observations in the sample*	*Percentage share of observations in the given size class in the sample (%)*	*Average number of non-financial enterprises in the given size class in the Polish economy (2018–2022)*	*Average percentage share of non-financial enterprises in the given size class in the Polish economy (2018–2022) (%)*
Micro-enterprises (0–9)	53,719	30.15	2197874,60	97.00
Small enterprises (10–49)	72,937	40.94	49607,00	2.19
Medium-sized enterprises (50–249)	39,607	22.23	14676,40	0.65
Large enterprises (over 250)	11,900	6.68	3719,25	0.1
Total	178,163	100	2265877,25	100.00

Source: Own elaboration based on original research and the Local Data Bank (Statistics Poland – Local Data Bank, 2024).

of the research sample is consistent with the general enterprise population structure in terms of the dominance of micro and small enterprises over medium and large ones, and the overwhelming prevalence of micro, small, and medium enterprises compared to large firms.

The total number of unique enterprises in the sample is 43,714. Due to changes in firm size classification during the study period, their count by size class and percentage share in the sample are not reported. The structure of the research sample used in this study also has an advantage over the samples used by GUS, which do not include microenterprises. The inclusion of microenterprises is a significant strength of this research, as they represent 97% of all non-financial enterprises in Poland, and therefore their cumulative contribution to the country's added value is considerable.

Statistics Poland has been conducting research on enterprise growth since 2011, when pilot studies were first carried out. Initially, these were conducted at the national level, but later analyses were also conducted at the voivodeship level. GUS carries out these studies on a group of active enterprises with more than nine employees that maintain accounting records and submit annual enterprise surveys. In 2022, the research sample in the GUS study included 37,684 enterprises, which is smaller than the sample used in this study (GUS, 2011, 2024).

Table 3.5 presents the structure of the studied enterprises by size category based on employment, broken down by voivodeship, along with corresponding values for the population of non-financial enterprises.

The structure of enterprise size classes in the research sample accurately reflects the differences in the number of business entities between voivodeships in the total population. The distribution of size classes in the sample is similar to the distribution in the population.

Table 3.6 presents the structure of enterprises in the sample by organizational and legal form, along with a comparison to the total population.

The data presented in Table 3.6 show that there is an overrepresentation of limited liability companies in the sample compared to civil law partnerships. This is due to the fact that the vast majority of civil partnerships are not required to use full accounting, which limits their presence in the Orbis database. Table 3.7 presents the structure of enterprises by the main section of the PKD code in the sample and in the population.

Table 3.7 shows that enterprises in the sample fully represent the industries in which business activity is conducted in Poland. The distribution in the sample is relatively close to the distribution in the population.

Characteristics of sustainable high-growth enterprises

After conducting the data cleansing procedure described in Section 4.4, the share of high-growth enterprises (i.e., those with an average annual growth

Table 3.5 Structure of surveyed enterprises by size (employment) at the Voivodeship Level (average for 2018–2022) with comparison to the population

Region	*Number and share of non-financial enterprises in the Polish economy (0–9 employees) (%)*		*Number and share of non-financial enterprises registered in REGON in the Polish economy (10–49 employees) (%)*		*Number and share of non-financial enterprises registered in REGON in the Polish economy (50–249 employees) (%)*		*Number and share of non-financial enterprises registered in REGON in the Polish economy (over 250 employees) (%)*		*Number and share of observations for 0–9 employees (the sample) (%)*		*Number and share of observations for 10–49 employees (the sample) (%)*		*Number and share of observations for 50–249 employees (the sample) (%)*		*Number and share of observations for over 250 employees (the sample) (%)*	
Dolnośląskie	16982.0	7.716	3661.2	7.380	1109.8	7.562	338.75	9.108	5362	9.98	6376	8.74	3140	7.93	1140	9.58
Kujawsko-Pomorskie	108251.2	4.925	2436.2	4.911	735.0	5.008	171	4.598	1882	3.50	3355	4.60	2082	5.26	510	4.30
Lubelskie	90512.6	4.118	2012.8	4.057	511.8	3.487	93.75	2.521	1690	3.14	2396	3.28	1180	2.98	238	2.0
Lubuskie	50745.2	2.309	1193.0	2.405	362.4	2.469	85.25	2.292	929	1.73	1568	2.15	1058	2.67	329	2.76
Łódzkie	125751.2	5.721	2996.6	6.041	886.8	6.042	196.75	5.290	1765	3.28	3262	4.47	2225	5.62	568	4.78
Małopolskie	231457.6	10.531	4810.4	9.697	1290.4	8.792	288	7.743	4258	7.93	6451	8.84	3244	8.19	901	7.54
Mazowieckie	410564.0	18.680	8176.4	16.482	2692.6	18.346	901.75	24.245	15057	28.03	15599	21.387	7544	19.05	2926	24.61
Opolskie	43271.2	1.969	1146.2	2.311	318.4	2.169	76.25	2.050	1107	2.06	1700	2.33	888	2.24	259	2.18
Podkarpackie	88411.4	4.023	2437.0	4.913	689.8	4.700	149	4.006	936	1.74	2350	3.22	1725	4.36	504	4.22
Podlaskie	57001.4	2.593	1201.6	2.4225	365.4	2.490	64.25	1.727	954	1.78	1654	2.27	951	2.40	178	1.49
Pomorskie	148403.2	6.752%	3202.6	6.456	959.8	6.540	228.5	06.233	5103	9.50	5622	7.71	2810	7.09	761	6.40
Śląskie	234116.4	10.652	6500.0	13.103	1819.4	12.397	472,75	12.711	4739	8.82	8347	11.44	4805	12.13	1557	13.11
Świętokrzyskie	53415.0	2.430	1236.4	2.492	332.4	2.265	80.75	2.171	721	1.34	1298	1.78	783	1.98	203	1.71
Warmińsko-Mazurskie	64927.8	2.954	1353.4	2.728	430.6	2.934	73.5	1.976	1133	2.11	1739	2.38	1077	2.72	218	1.82
Wielkopolskie	214794.6	9.773	5392.4	10.870	1,620.8	11.044	405	10.889	5806	10.81	8219	11.27	4517	11.40	1293	10.87
Zachodniopomorskie	106669.8	4.853	1850.8	3.731	551,0	3.754	94	2.527	2277	4.24	3001	4.11	1578	3.98	315	2,63
Razem	2197874.6	100	49607.0	100	14,676.4	100	3719,25	100.00	53719	100.00	72937	100.00	39607	100.00	11900	100,00

Source: Own elaboration based on original research and the Local Data Bank (Statistics Poland – Local Data Bank, 2024).

Table 3.6 Structure of surveyed enterprises by legal-organizational form compared to the structure of non-financial entities in the REGON register conducting business activity

Legal form	*Number of enterprises in the sample*	*%*	*Number of observations in the sample*	*%*	*Number of registered legal entities and organizational units without legal personality in REGON (2023)*	*%*
Limited liability company (Sp. z o.o.)	35,200	80.52	143,381	80.48	576,340	60.22
Joint stock company (S.A.)	2,368	5.41	10,438	5.85	9,641	1.00
Limited partnership	2,583	5.91	10,363	5.82	36,744	3.84
Registered partnership	3,103	7.1	12,731	7.14	34,041	3.56
Civil law partnership	7	0.02	7	0	291,610	30.47
Limited joint-stock partnership	186	0.42	733	0.41	3,952	0.41
European company	3	0.01	12	0.01	No data	-
State-owned enterprise	7	0.02	31	0.02	39	0.0041
Professional partnership	34	0.08	141	0.08	2,471	0.26
Simple joint stock company	30	0,07	121	0.07	2,195	0.23
Sole proprietorship	193	0.44	205	0.12	-	-
Total	43,714	100	178,163	100	957,033	100

Source: Own elaboration based on original research and the Local Data Bank (Statistics Poland – Local Data Bank, 2024).

Table 3.7 Structure of surveyed enterprises and the population by section of the main PKD Code

PKD section	*Section description*	*Number of enterprises in the sample*	*%*	*Number of observations in the sample*	*%*	*Number of enterprises in the population*	*%*
A	Agriculture, forestry, hunting and fishing	992	2.27	3,733	2.10	14,460	1.17
B	Mining and quarrying	199	0.43	811	0.46	2,094	0.16
C	Manufacturing	9,685	22.16	41,563	23.33	93,018	7.49
D	Electricity, gas, steam, hot water and air conditioning supply	475	1.09	2,045	1.15	11,302	0.91
E	Water supply; sewerage, waste management and remediation activities	1,115	2.55	5,113	2.87	5,033	0.40
F	Construction	3,846	8.80	15,502	8.70	97,818	7.88
G	Wholesale and retail trade; repair of motor vehicles and motorcycles	11,506	26.32	47,557	26.69	238,466	19.21
H	Transportation and storage	2,048	4.68	8,539	4.79	42,418	3.41
I	Accommodation and food service activities	1,015	2.32	3,627	2.04	39,853	3,21
J	Information and communication	2,310	5.28	9,140	5.13	46,572	3.75
K	Financial and insurance activities	793	1.82	3,046	1.71	29,183	2.35
L	Real estate activities	2,279	5.21	8,739	4.91	197,214	15.89
M	Professional, scientific and technical activities	3,755	8.59	14,293	8.02	102,926	8.29
N	Administrative and support service activities	1,557	3.56	6,099	3.42	41,523	3.34
O	Public administration and defence; compulsory social security	10	0.02	38	0.02	16,109	1.30
P	Education	341	0.79	1,195	0.67	35,177	2.83
Q	Human health and social work activities	1,339	3.07	5,389	3.01	21,919	1.77
R	Arts, entertainment and recreation	266	0.62	991	0.56	40,257	3.24
S	Other service activities	183	0.42	743	0.42	165,309	13.32
T	Households as employers; undifferentiated goods- and services-producing activities of households for own use	0	0	0	0		
U	Extraterritorial organizations and bodies	0	0	0	0	269	0.021
Total	-	43,714	100	178,163	100	1240,920	100

Source: Own elaboration based on original research and the Local Data Bank (Statistics Poland – Local Data Bank, 2024).

rate of 20% over the past three years) amounted to 5,593 observations, which represents 3.14% of the research sample.

From among these high-growth enterprise observations, those classified as sustainable high-growth enterprises were identified as those in the top 25% each year in terms of ROE, solvency, liquidity, and employment growth. After applying this criterion, 1,638 observations remained (representing 1,428 unique entities). Most sustainable high-growth enterprises recorded sustainable high growth only once.

In the research sample, 28,531 companies (65.27%) had a PKD code listed in the KRS or CEIDG registers that, according to Eurostat classification, qualify as either high-tech knowledge-intensive services (for service companies) or as high-technology or medium-high-technology (for manufacturing companies). A knowledge-intensive PKD code appeared as the main activity for 9,577 companies, representing 21.91% of all enterprises in the sample. Among sustainable high-growth enterprises, 1,017 companies (71.21%) engaged in knowledge-intensive activities, and for 411 of them (28.78%), it was their main line of business. Additionally, the average company in the sample carried out three types of knowledge-intensive activities, while for SHG companies, the average was four knowledge-intensive activities.

The average scope of operations, measured by the number of activity types conducted by a company, was 21 for all companies in the sample and 22 for sustainable high-growth enterprises, indicating that SHG enterprises were less specialized in their operations. Table 3.8 presents the number of companies and observations of SHG enterprises, as well as their share across different size classes.

The total number of SHG observations is 1,638. Micro-enterprises accounted for 47.86% of this set (784 observations), small enterprises 37.06% (607 observations), medium-sized enterprises 13.00% (213 observations), and large enterprises 2.07% (34 observations). The structure is similar to the overall sample, with micro and small enterprises dominating, and significantly fewer medium and large enterprises.

The number of unique SHG enterprises is 1,428. Due to changes in enterprise size class over time, the number and share of enterprises by size class

Table 3.8 Characteristics of sustainable high-growth enterprises by size class

Size class (number of employees)	*Number of observations*	*%*
Micro-enterprises (0–9)	784	47.86
Small enterprises (10–49)	607	37.07
Medium-sized enterprises (50–249)	213	13.00
Large enterprises (more than 250)	34	2.07
Total	1638	100

Source: Own research.

Table 3.9 Structure of sustainable high-growth enterprises by employment size class and region

Voivodeship/size class	*Number of micro-enterprises*	*%*	*Number of small enterprises*	*%*	*Number of medium-sized enterprises*	*%*	*Number of large enterprises*	*%*
Dolnośląskie	76	9.69	58	9.56	17	7.98	2	5.88
Kujawsko-Pomorskie	21	2.67	27	4.45	9	4.23	0	0
Lubelskie	34	4.33	22	3.62	4	1.88	0	0
Lubuskie	11	1.40	11	1.81	6	2.82	1	2.94
Łódzkie	26	3.32	23	3.79	11	5.16	1	2.94
Małopolskie	46	5.87	54	8.90	17	7.98	3	8.82
Mazowieckie	261	33.29	149	24.55	52	24.41	12	35.30
Opolskie	10	1.28	11	1.81	4	1.88	1	2.94
Podkarpackie	11	1.40	21	3.46	7	3.29	2	5.88
Podlaskie	13	1.66	14	2.31	10	4.69	0	0
Pomorskie	83	10.59	52	8.57	20	9.39	8	23.54
Śląskie	69	8.80	64	10.54	30	14.08	2	5.88
Świętokrzyskie	4	0.51	7	1.16	3	1.41	0	0
Warmińsko-Mazurskie	15	1.91	11	1.81	4	1.88	1	2.94
Wielkopolskie	67	8.55	61	10.04	17	7.98	1	2.94
Zachodniopomorskie	37	4.3	22	3.62	2	0.94	0	0
Total	784	100	607	100	213	100	34	100

Source: Own research.

are not provided. The majority of SHG enterprises did not maintain SHG in the subsequent period – this share is comparable to that of high-growth enterprises. Table 3.9 presents the size structure of SHG enterprises by regions.

The size structure of SHG enterprises at the voivodeship level differs significantly from the equivalent structure in the overall population. Due to size class changes over time, Table 3.9 reports observations rather than unique entities. There are no large SHG enterprises in the Świętokrzyskie, Podlaskie, and West Pomeranian voivodeships, while over 50% are located in the Mazowieckie and Pomorskie voivodeships. Table 3.10 presents the number and share of different legal forms of SHG enterprises within the total SHG dataset.

As with the enterprise sample and population, Table 3.11 shows the dominant share of limited liability companies, which – together with joint-stock and limited partnerships – constitute over 97% of the SHG population. There are no entities registered in the CEIDG. Table 3.11 shows the structure of SHG enterprises by section of the main PKD code.

The enterprises represent nearly all industry groups, with the exception of section "O," which includes compulsory social security, public administration, and national defense. Table 3.12 presents the share of SHG in the sample by year and region.

The data show that for the years 2019–2022, the share of SHG remained relatively stable. Higher shares of SHG across various regions were observed for the year 2018. A similar pattern is also visible for high-growth enterprises. The ratio of high-growth enterprises to SHG is roughly proportional across individual EEs.

Table 3.10 Structure of sustainable high-growth enterprises by legal and organizational form

Legal and organizational form	*Number of enterprises*	*%*	*Number of observations*	*%*
Limited liability company	1,198	83.89	1,378	84.12
Joint-stock company	92	6.45	104	6.35
Limited partnership	97	6.79	111	6.78
Registered partnership	33	2.31	35	2.14
Civil law partnership	0	0	0	0
Limited joint-stock partnership	7	0.49	9	0.55
European company	0	0	0	0
State-owned enterprise	0	0	0	0
Professional partnership	1	0.07	1	0.06
Simple joint-stock company	0	0	0	0
Sole proprietorship	0	0	0	0
Total	1,428	100	1,638	100

Source: Own research.

Table 3.11 Structure of sustainable high-growth enterprises by section of the main PKD code

PKD Section	*Section description*	*Number of sustainable high-growth enterprises*	*%*	*Number of observations*	*%*
A	Agriculture, forestry, hunting, and fishing	25	1.75	26	1.59
B	Mining and quarrying	8	0.56	9	0.55
C	Manufacturing	208	14.57	244	14.90
D	Electricity, gas, steam, and air conditioning supply	16	1.12	17	1.04
E	Water supply; sewerage, waste management, and remediation activities	33	2.31	40	2.44
F	Construction	243	17.03	277	16.91
G	Wholesale and retail trade; repair of motor vehicles and motorcycles	208	14.57	238	14.53
H	Transportation and storage	68	4.76	80	4.88
I	Accommodation and food service activities	47	3.29	53	3.24
J	Information and communication	108	7.56	133	8.12
K	Financial and insurance activities	46	3.22	52	3.17
L	Real estate activities	94	6.58	101	6.17
M	Professional, scientific, and technical activities	184	12.88	213	13.00
N	Administrative and support service activities	69	4.83	77	4.70
O	Public administration and defense; compulsory social security	0	0	0	0
P	Education	27	1.89	29	1.77
Q	Human health and social work activities	24	1.68	28	1.71
R	Arts, entertainment, and recreation	12	0.84	12	0.73
S	Other service activities	8	0.56	9	0.55
T	Households employing domestic staff; undifferentiated goods- and services-producing activities of private households for own use	0	0	0	0
U	Extraterritorial organizations and bodies	0	0	0	0
Total	-	1,428	100	1,638	100

Source: Own research.

Table 3.12 Share of sustainable high-growth enterprises in the sample by year and voivodeship

Voivodeship/year	*2018 (%)*	*2019 (%)*	*2020 (%)*	*2021 (%)*	*2022 (%)*	*Average for the years 2018–2022 (%)*
Mazowieckie	1.51	0.93	1.04	0.85	1.49	1.16
Pomorskie	1.71	0.90	0.78	0.84	1.56	1.16
Lubelskie	2.19	0.80	1.31	0.54	0.66	1.11
Podlaskie	2.00	0.91	0.90	0.52	0.69	1.00
Dolnośląskie	1.35	0.70	0.78	0.82	1.15	0.96
Śląskie	1.14	0.74	0.85	0.53	1.00	0.85
Zachodniopomorskie	0.81	1.02	0.68	0.88	0.86	0.85
Małopolskie	1.30	0.53	0.68	0.68	0.90	0.82
Łódzkie	0.75	0.50	0.74	0.93	0.98	0.78
Lubuskie	0.97	0.50	0.74	0.50	1.07	0.76
Podkarpackie	1.16	0.62	0.52	0.44	1.02	0.75
Warmińsko-Mazurskie	1.17	0.94	0.59	0.57	0.49	0.76
Wielkopolskie	1.01	0.37	0.76	0.78	0.78	0.74
Kujawsko Pomorskie	1.00	0.50	0.74	0.62	0.78	0.73
Opolskie	1.18	0.12	0.25	0.97	0.79	0.66
Świętokrzyskie	0.36	0.16	0.65	0.63	0.50	0.46

Source: Own research.

Bibliography

Anselin, L. (1995). Local Indicators of Spatial Association—LISA. *Geographical Analysis*, *27*(2), 93–115. https://doi.org/10.1111/j.1538-4632.1995.tb00338.x

Anselin, L., & Li, X. (2020). Tobler's law in a multivariate world. *Geographical Analysis*, *52*(4), 494–510. https://doi.org/10.1111/gean.12237

Ashraf, S. N., & Singh, A. K. (2019). Does entrepreneurship ecosystem have a long-term relationship with economic growth in selected economies? A statistical investigation. *Proceedings of the 13th Biennial Conference on Entrepreneurship Organized by EDII Ahmedabad*, *1*, 176–187. https://www.researchgate.net/profile/Ajay-Singh-165/publication/344326215_Does_entrepreneurship_ecosystem_have_a_long-term_relationship_with_economic_Growth_in_selected_economies_A_statistical_investigation/links/5f682dc892851c14bc8bcceb/Does-entrepreneurship-ecosystem-have-a-long-term-relationship-with-economic-Growth-in-selected-economies-A-statistical-investigation.pdf

Baumol, W. J. (1996). Entrepreneurship: Productive, unproductive, and destructive. *Journal of Business Venturing*, *11*(1), 3–22.

Bejjani, M., Göcke, L., & Menter, M. (2023). Digital entrepreneurial ecosystems: A systematic literature review. *Technological Forecasting and Social Change*, *189*, 122372.

Bland, J. R., & Cook, A. C. (2019). Random effects probit and logit: Understanding predictions and marginal effects. *Applied Economics Letters*, *26*(2), 116–123. https://doi.org/10.1080/13504851.2018.1441498

Bouncken, R. B., & Kraus, S. (2022). Entrepreneurial ecosystems in an interconnected world: Emergence, governance and digitalization. *Review of Managerial Science, 16*(1), 1–14. https://doi.org/10.1007/s11846-021-00444-1

Charles, V., & Zegarra, L. F. (2014). Measuring regional competitiveness through data envelopment analysis: A Peruvian case. *Expert Systems with Applications, 41*(11), 5371–5381.

Chen, Y. (2013). New approaches for calculating Moran's index of spatial autocorrelation. *PloS One, 8*(7), e68336.

Elia, G., Margherita, A., & Passiante, G. (2020). Digital entrepreneurship ecosystem: How digital technologies and collective intelligence are reshaping the entrepreneurial process. *Technological Forecasting and Social Change, 150*, 119791.

Foster, G., Shimizu, C., Ciesinski, S., Davila, A., Hassan, S., Jia, N., & Morris, R. (2013). Entrepreneurial ecosystems around the globe and company growth dynamics. *World Economic Forum, 11*(2), 145–159.

Gancarczyk, M. (2017). *The process of SME growth: Integrating the resource-based and transaction cost approaches*. Jagiellonian University Press.

Gancarczyk, M., & Konopa, S. (2021). Exploring the governance of entrepreneurial ecosystems for productive high growth. *Foresight and STI Governance, 15*(4), 9–21.

Gomes, S., Ferreira, J. J., & Lopes, J. M. (2023). Entrepreneurial conditions and economic growth in entrepreneurial ecosystems: Evidence from OECD countries. *The International Journal of Entrepreneurship and Innovation, 26*(4), 315–333. https://doi.org/10.1177/14657503231156340

Greene, W. (2010). Testing hypotheses about interaction terms in nonlinear models. *Economics Letters, 107*(2), 291–296.

Hartman, J. B., & Kear, M. T. (2024). Governing by entrepreneurship: Entrepreneurial ecosystems and socio-spatial difference. *Competition & Change, 28*(1), 209–227. https://doi.org/10.1177/10245294231180297

Isenberg, D. (2011). *The Entrepreneurship Ecosystem Strategy as a New Paradigm for Economic Policy: Principles for Cultivating Entrepreneurship*, Institute of International and European Affairs, Dublin, Ireland, 12 May 2011, 1–13.

Krugman, P. (1991). Increasing returns and economic geography. *Journal of Political Economy, 99*(3), 483–499. https://doi.org/10.1086/261763

Liguori, E., Bendickson, J., Solomon, S., & McDowell, W. C. (2019). Development of a multi-dimensional measure for assessing entrepreneurial ecosystems. *Entrepreneurship & Regional Development, 31*(1–2), 7–21. https://doi.org/10.1080/08985626.2018.1537144

Mason, C., & Brown, R. (2010). *High growth firms in Scotland*. https://strathprints.strath.ac.uk/28232/

Miller, H. J. (2004). Tobler's first law and spatial analysis. *Annals of the Association of American Geographers, 94*(2), 284–289. https://doi.org/10.1111/j.1467-8306.2004.09402005.x

Mitra, S., Kumar, H., Gupta, M. P., & Bhattacharya, J. (2023). Entrepreneurship in smart cities: Elements of start-up ecosystem. *Journal of Science and Technology Policy Management, 14*(3), 592–611.

Nelson, H. P., Devenish-Nelson, E. S., Rusk, B. L., Geary, M., & Lawrence, A. J. (2020). A review of tropical dry forest ecosystem service research in the Caribbean – gaps and policy-implications. *Ecosystem Services, 43*, 101095. https://doi.org/10.1016/j.ecoser.2020.101095

Nelson, R. R., & Winter, S. G. (1973). Toward an evolutionary theory of economic capabilities. *The American Economic Review*, *63*(2), 440–449.

Panzar, J. C., & Willig, R. D. (1981). Economies of scope. *The American Economic Review*, *71*(2), 268–272.

Penrose, E. (1959). *Theory of the growth*. John Wiley & Sons.

Putnam, R. D. (1995). Tuning in, tuning out: The strange disappearance of social capital in America. *PS: Political Science & Politics*, *28*(4), 664–683.

Singh, A. K., Kumar, S., & Jyoti, B. (2023). Does entrepreneurship ecosystem have a causal relationship with economic development? A country-wise imbalanced panel data investigation. In Magd, H. Khan, S. A. Nte, N. D., & Sarim M (Eds.), *Entrepreneurship and economic sustainability*, Prestige Publishers, New Delhi, 1–15.

Stam, E., & Van De Ven, A. (2021). Entrepreneurial ecosystem elements. *Small Business Economics*, *56*(2), 809–832. https://doi.org/10.1007/s11187-019-00270-6

Sui, D. Z. (2004). Tobler's first law of geography: A big idea for a small world? *Annals of the Association of American Geographers*, *94*(2), 269–277. https://doi.org/10.1111/j.1467-8306.2004.09402003.x

Suresh, J., & Ramraj, R. (2012). Entrepreneurial ecosystem: Case study on the influence of environmental factors on entrepreneurial success. *European Journal of Business and Management*, *4*(16), 95–101.

Teece, D. J. (1980). Economies of scope and the scope of the enterprise. *Journal of Economic Behavior & Organization*, *1*(3), 223–247.

Teece, D. J. (1997). Economies of scope and the scope of the enterprise. *Resources, Firms and Strategies*, 103–116.

Torres, P., & Godinho, P. (2022). Levels of necessity of entrepreneurial ecosystems elements. *Small Business Economics*, *59*(1), 29–45. https://doi.org/10.1007/s11187-021-00515-3

Williamson, O. E. (1971). The vertical integration of production: Market failure considerations. *The American Economic Review*, *61*(2), 112–123.

4 Regional entrepreneurial ecosystems and sustainable entrepreneurship in Poland against international experience

4.1 Characteristics of entrepreneurial ecosystems and sustainable high growth of enterprises in Poland

A series of panel logistic models were used to analyze the impact of entrepreneurship ecosystem (EE) dimensions on the likelihood of achieving sustainable high growth (SHG). These models included control variables, resource-based factors, and optimally weighted variables representing the dimensions of ecosystems or an aggregated EE index. Backward stepwise regression was applied to identify the final set of variables. To verify Hypothesis H1, stating that SHG of enterprises depends on the structural characteristics of EEs, a random-effects panel logistic regression was performed, incorporating the results of spectral cluster analysis that identified the membership of ecosystems in groups with differentiated characteristics.

The scree plot (Figure 4.1) indicated two clusters as the optimal number. The first cluster (coded as "1") included the Mazowieckie and Małopolskie regions, while the second cluster comprised the remaining voivodeships.

EEs belonging to Cluster 1 show higher parameters across all ecosystem dimensions; in the case of physical infrastructure and human resource competency dimensions, these can be considered outliers. The results of Model 1, which accounts for the structural differentiation of enterprises and its impact on sustainable growth, are presented in Table 4.1.

The results of the likelihood ratio test (testing whether the rho coefficient equals zero) indicate that it is more appropriate to use a panel model than a standard logistic regression. An artificial variable representing clusters was added to the tested variables. After performing the stepwise backward regression, the following variables were found to be statistically significant: two synthetic EE variables describing the dimensions of human resource competencies and knowledge development and research activity, resource variables such as firm age, industry knowledge intensity, and prior sustainable high, as well as spatial interactions and urbanization. Synthetic variables representing other EE dimensions – such as physical infrastructure, digital economy, and access to finance and institutional quality – along with firm size and the GDP of the EE, proved to be statistically insignificant.

DOI: 10.4324/9781003739333-5

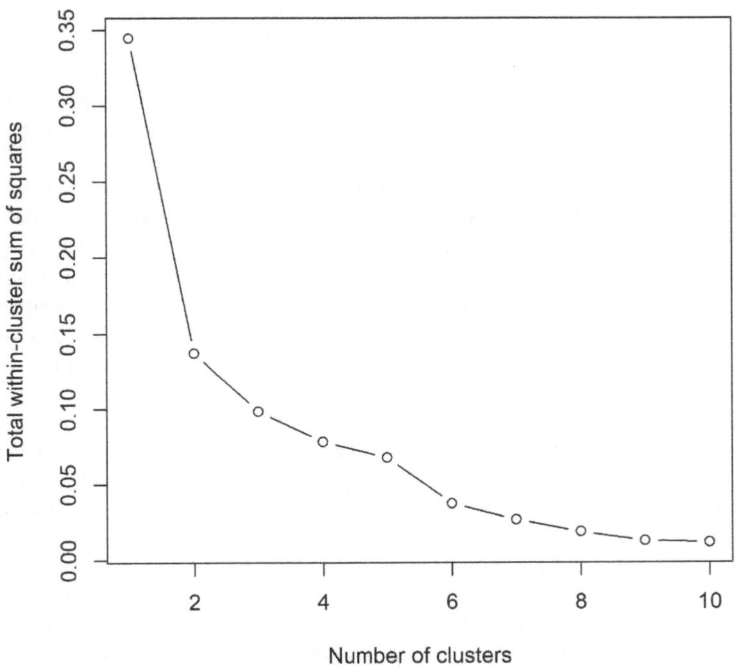

Figure 4.1 Scree plot showing the optimal number of clusters

Table 4.1 Results of model 1 highlighting the impact of EE dimensions on the probability of achieving SHG, taking into account the structural diversity of the EE

Variable/ parameter	*Odds ratio*	*Std. err*	*Z*	*P>|z|*	*[95% conf. interval]*	
Age	0.9451367	0.0035537	−15.01	0.000	0.9381973	0.9521275
Know	1.014546	0.0036454	4.02	0.000	1.007426	1.021716
Urb	1.005178	0.0010072	5.15	0.000	1.003206	1.007154
SHGt1	11.23955	2.44971	11.10	0.000	7.332056	17.22948
SHGin	1.860099	0.1870665	6.17	0.000	1.527328	2.265373
Hc	1.164667	0.0395676	4.49	0.000	1.089642	1.244859
Rd	1.107473	0.0342055	3.31	0.001	1.042421	1.176586
Clust	0.6881689	0.0797908	−3.22	0.001	0.5482785	0.8637517
_cons	0.0062015	0.0010594	−29.76	0.000	0.004437	0.0086676
/lnsig2u	−0.3470367	0.3479484			−1.029003	0.3349297
sigma_u	0.8407017	0.1462604			0.5977985	1.182304
rho	0.1768431	0.0506507			0.097982	0.2981929
LR test of rho=0 = 9.2	Prob > 0.001					

Source: Own calculation.

Enterprises that held the status of SHG enterprises in the previous year have a 1,023.96% higher chance of achieving HG next year. An increase of one percentage point in the share of SHG enterprises in neighboring ecosystems increases the probability of SHG by 86.01%, while an increase of one unit in the human resource competency dimension index raises this probability by 16.47%.

An increase of one unit in the knowledge development and research activity index raises the probability by 10.75%, and each additional knowledge-intensive activity in a firm's portfolio increases the likelihood of achieving SHG status by 1.49%. Increasing the level of local urbanization by one percentage point raises the probability of SHG by 0.52%. The opposite effect is observed for firm age – each additional year reduces the probability of SHG by 5.49%. Enterprises located within EEs belonging to cluster 1 have a 31.18% lower probability of achieving SHG compared to other firms, assuming all other factors remain constant.

To examine whether structural differentiation affects SHGE at the level of the aggregate EE, the results of the spectral cluster analysis, showing EE membership in groups with differentiated characteristics, were included in Model 2 (Table 4.2).

The results of the likelihood ratio test (testing whether the rho coefficient equals zero) indicate that it is more appropriate to use a panel model than a standard logistic regression. A synthetic variable representing clusters was added to the tested variables. After performing the stepwise backward regression, the following variables were found to be statistically significant: the

Table 4.2 Results of model 2 highlighting the impact of the aggregated EE index on the probability of achieving SHG, taking into account the structural diversity of the EE

Variable/ parameter	*Odds ratio*	*Std. err*	*Z*	*P>|z|*	*[95% conf. interval]*	
Age	0.9446917	0.0035443	−15.17	0.000	0.9377705	0.951664
Know	1.01469	0.0036397	4.07	0.000	1.007581	1.021849
Urb	1.005252	0.0010077	5.23	0.000	1.003279	1.007229
SHGt1	10.89844	2.375188	10.96	0.000	7.109761	16.70605
SHGin	1.867039	0.189254	6.16	0.000	1.530632	2.277384
Clust	0.8127123	0.075333	−2.24	0.025	0.6776979	0.9746249
Agr_ee	1.133003	0.0307376	4.60	0.000	1.074332	1.194878
_cons	0.0061278	0.0010646	−29.33	0.000	0.0043594	0.0086135
/lnsig2u	−0.313762	0.3387947			−0.9777875	0.3502634
sigma_u	0.8548058	0.1448018			0.6133045	1.191403
rho	.181739	0.503821			0.1026027	0.3014118
LR test of rho=0 = 9.74	Prob > 0.001					

Source: Own calculation.

aggregate EE index, the EE structure affiliation, resource variables including firm age, industry knowledge intensity, and prior SHG, as well as urbanization and spatial interaction indicators. Variables such as firm size, scope of activity, and EE GDP were statistically insignificant.

Enterprises with SHG status in the previous period have a 989.84% higher chance of achieving SHG in the next period. An increase of one percentage point in the share of SHG firms in neighboring ecosystems increases the probability of SHG by 86.70%, an increase of one unit in the aggregate EE index raises this probability by 13.30%, each additional knowledge-intensive activity increases the likelihood of achieving SHG by 1.47%, and a one-percentage-point increase in local urbanization raises the probability of SHG by 0.53%. Conversely, each additional year of firm age reduces the probability of SHG by 5.53%. Enterprises located within EEs belonging to cluster 1 have an 18.72% lower chance of SHG compared to other firms, assuming all other factors remain constant.

Model 1 confirmed Hypothesis H1 at the level of EE dimensions, while Model 2 confirmed it at the level of the aggregate EE index. This indicates that SHG depends on the structural characteristics of EEs, both at the level of individual ecosystem dimensions and at the level of the aggregate index. Incorporating structural differentiation improves the explanatory power of the model at both levels of analysis.

4.2 Enterprise heterogeneity as a moderator of the impact of Polish entrepreneurial ecosystems on the SHG of enterprises

The next aspect examined is the moderating effect of enterprise heterogeneity on the impact of EEs on SHG of enterprises. First, Hypothesis H2.1, which posits the moderation effects of firm characteristics on EE, will be tested. The marginal effects in this section were calculated based on panel logistic regressions constructed according to the formula described in Chapter 3. That is, in Model 1 and Model 2, an interaction term between the firm resource variable and the ecosystem dimension, or its aggregate index, was added.

To verify H2.1, models 3a–3f were defined. Model 3a is designed to examine whether firm age moderates the impact of the aggregate EE index on SHG.

Model 3a: SHG ~ age + know + *urb* + SHG*t*1 + SHG*in* + *clust* + *agr*_ee + *int*_agr_ee_age (26)

where the symbol ~ denotes "depends on the following variables."

This notation was used to simplify the representation of the panel logistic regression.

Marginal effects are calculated from the minimum to the maximum values of the variables.

Model 3b is designed to examine whether firm age moderates the impact of the human resource competency dimension on SHG of enterprises.

$$Model\ 3b: SHG \sim age + know + urb + SHGt1 + SHGin + clust + hc + rd + int\_hc\_age \quad (27)$$

Model 3c is designed to examine whether firm age moderates the impact of the knowledge development and research activity dimension on SHG.

$$Model\ 3c: SHG \sim age + know + urb + SHGt1 + SHGin + clust + hc + rd + int\_rd\_age \quad (28)$$

Model 3d is designed to examine whether the knowledge intensity of the firm's activity moderates the impact of the aggregate EE on SHG.

$$Model\ 3d: SHG \sim age + know + urb + SHGt1 + SHGin + clust + agr\_ee + int\_agr\_ee\_know \quad (29)$$

Model 3e is designed to examine whether the knowledge intensity of a firm's activities moderates the impact of the human resource competency dimension on SHG.

$$Model\ 3e: SHG \sim age + know + urb + SHGt1 + SHGin + clust + hc + rd + int\_hc\_know \quad (30)$$

Model 3f is designed to examine whether the knowledge intensity of activity moderates the impact of the knowledge development and research activity dimension on SHG.

$$Model\ 3f: SHG \sim age + know + urb + SHGt1 + SHGin + clust + hc + ed + int\_ed\_know \quad (31)$$

Figure 4.2 presents a visualization of the average marginal effects. The letter labels in the figures correspond to the variants of model 3.

Analysis of marginal effects from models 3a–3f, the results of which are illustrated in Figure 4.2, shows several relationships. Model 3a indicates that the aggregated EE has a stronger positive effect the younger the enterprise is, and this effect diminishes with firm age. Marginal effects are significant only for the first four values, that is, for firms up to 15 years old and younger. Model 3b shows that the human resource competence dimension has the

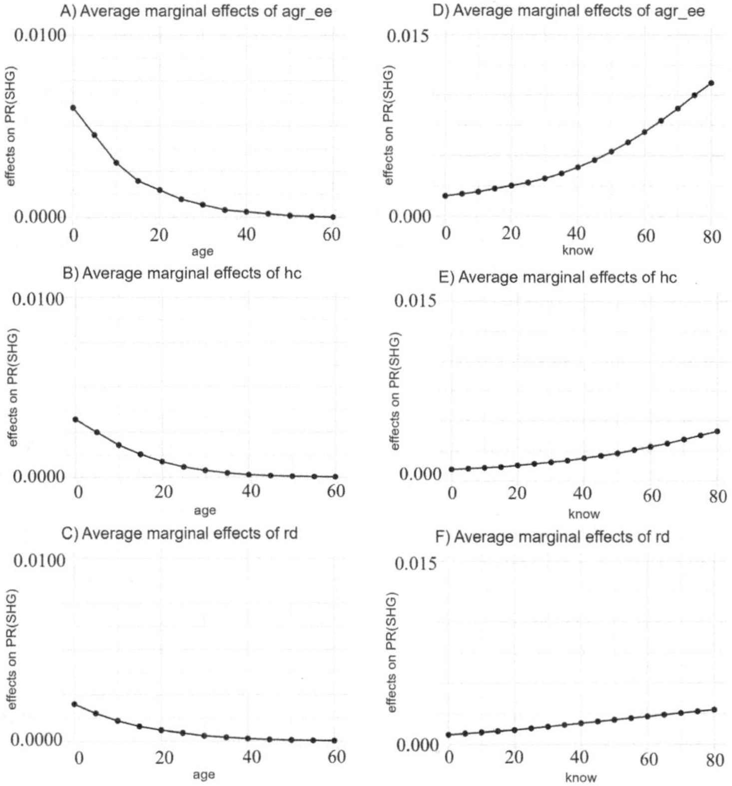

Figure 4.2 Average marginal effects of (a), (d) the aggregated EE index, (b), (e) the human resources competence dimension, (c), (f) at representative values of (a), (b), (c) age and (d), (e), (f) industry knowledge intensity

greatest and most positive impact on the youngest enterprises, and this effect decreases as the firm's age increases. Marginal effects are significant for all firm age values.

Model 3c shows that the knowledge development and research activity dimension has the strongest positive impact on the youngest enterprises, and the magnitude of this effect declines as the firms get older. However, the marginal effects are statistically insignificant for the firm age variable. Model 3d shows that the positive impact of the aggregated EE increases with the number of knowledge-intensive activities conducted by the enterprise. Marginal effects are statistically significant only for the first six values, that is, for firms engaged in up to 25 knowledge-intensive activities.

Model 3e shows that the positive impact of the human resource competence dimension increases with the number of knowledge-intensive activities undertaken by the enterprise. Marginal effects are statistically significant for every number of knowledge-intensive activities in the firm's portfolio. Model 3f shows that the positive impact of the human resource competence dimension increases with the number of knowledge-intensive activities conducted by the enterprise. Marginal effects are statistically significant for every number of knowledge-intensive activities in which the enterprise is involved.

Based on models 3a–3f, hypothesis H2.1 should be positively verified – the impact of entrepreneurial ecosystems on SHG is moderated by firm characteristics such as age and the knowledge intensity of their activities. In the case of firm age, this effect is observed for both the overall ecosystem level (aggregated EE index) and the human resource competence dimension. The moderating effect of industry knowledge intensity of activity is also confirmed for the knowledge development and research activity dimension. Firm size and scope of operations have no statistically significant impact on SHG, and therefore do not exert a moderating effect. To estimate the marginal effects of the presence or absence of SHG in the prior year, models 4a, 4b, and 4c were used.

Model 4a is designed to examine whether prior SHG moderates the impact of aggregate EE on SHG.

Model 4*a*: *SHG ~ age + know + urb + SHGt1 + SHGin+ clust + agr_ee +*
+ agr_ee_SHGt1 (32)

Model 4b aims to examine whether prior productive growth is a moderating factor in the relationship between EEs and SHG enterprises.

Model 4*b*: *SHG ~ age + know + urb + SHGt1 + SHGin + hc + rd +*
int_hc_SHGt1 (33)

Model 4c is designed to examine whether prior growth moderates the impact of the knowledge development and research activity dimension on SHG.

Model 4*c*: *SHG ~ age + know + urb + SHGt1 + SHGin + clust + hc + rd*
+ int_rd_SHGt1 (34)

Figure 4.3 presents a visualization of the average marginal effects. The letter labels in the figures correspond to the variants of model 4.

Based on the marginal effects of models 4a–4c, Hypothesis H2.2 can be confirmed – prior SHG of enterprises is a moderator of the impact of EEs on SHG. This effect is visible at the level of the overall EE (aggregate index), the

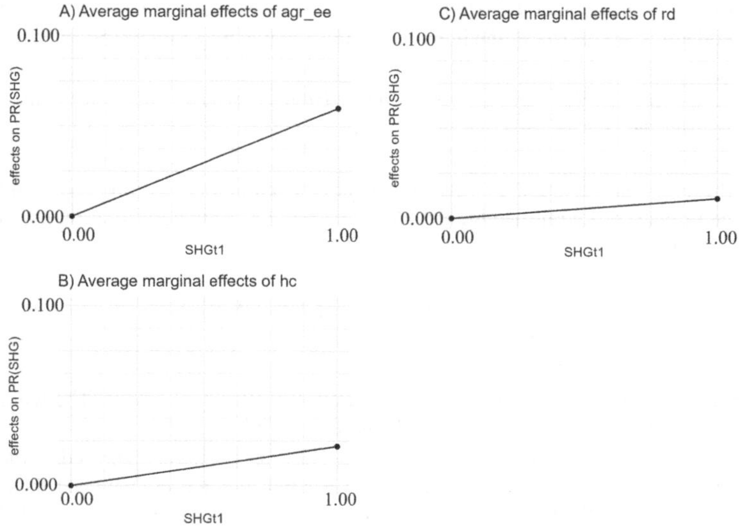

Figure 4.3 Average marginal effects of (a) aggregated EE index, (b) the human resources competence dimension, and (c) the knowledge and research activity development dimension at representative points of the prior sustainable high growth in the previous year

human resource competency dimension, and the knowledge development and research activity dimension.

Based on the marginal effects of Models 4a–4c and 3a–4f presented in the prior subsection, Hypothesis H2 can also be positively verified – heterogeneity of enterprises operating within EE moderates the impact of EE on SHG.

4.3 Spatial interactions as a moderator of the impact of Polish entrepreneurial ecosystems on the enterprise SHG

The next analysis concerns the moderation of the impact of EE on SHG by spatial interactions between ecosystems. Its aim is to verify the third hypothesis. For this purpose, Models 5a, 5b, and 5c were defined, and marginal effects were calculated. Model 5a is designed to examine whether spatial interactions moderate the impact of aggregate EE on SHG.

Model 5a: $SHG \sim age + know + urb + SHGt1 + SHGin + clust + agr\_ee + int\_agr\_ee\_SHGin$ (35)

Model 5b is designed to examine whether previous sustainable high growth moderates the impact of the human resource competency dimension on SHG.

$$\text{Model 5b: } SHG \sim age + know + urb + SHGt1 + SHGin + hc + rd + clust + int\_hc\_SHGin \quad (36)$$

Model 5c is designed to examine whether spatial interactions moderate the impact of the knowledge development and research activity dimension on SHG.

$$\text{Model 5c: } SHG \sim \mathrm{age} + \mathrm{know} + urb + SHGt1 + SHGin + hc + rd + clust + int\_rd\_SHGin \quad (37)$$

Figure 4.4 presents a visualization of the average marginal effects. The letter labels in the figures correspond to the variants of Model 5.

Based on Models 5a–5c, Hypothesis H3 was positively verified – the impact of EEs on SHG is moderated by spatial interactions between these ecosystems, both at the level of the overall EE and in terms of individual EE components.

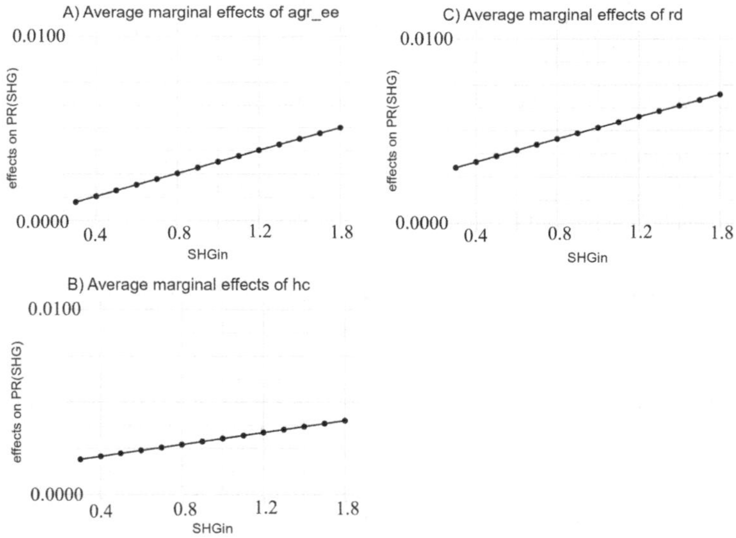

Figure 4.4 Average marginal effects of (a) aggregated EE index, (b) the human resources competence dimension, and (c) the knowledge and research activity development dimension at representative points of the average share of knowledge-intensive enterprises in neighboring EEs

4.4 Discussion and recommendations for business and economic policy in the context of international evidence

Summary of hypothesis verification

The analyses conducted allowed for the verification of the research hypotheses, summarized as follows:

H1. Sustainable high growth of enterprises depends on the structural characteristics of entrepreneurial ecosystems.

Model 1 indicated that the probability of achieving sustainable high growth is influenced by the human resource competency dimension and the knowledge development and research activity dimension. This model also showed that the variable introduced based on cluster analysis, representing the structural affiliation of EE, is statistically significant. Enterprises operating in the Mazowieckie and Małopolskie regions have a lower chance of achieving sustainable high growth than would be expected based on the characteristics of the human resource competency and knowledge development dimensions. Similarly, Model 2 shows that the statistical cluster variable has a similar effect for the aggregate EE index. Based on Models 1 and 2, H1 was positively verified for both individual dimensions and the aggregate EE index.

H2. The influence of entrepreneurial ecosystems on the sustainable high growth of firms is moderated by the heterogeneity of the companies operating within these ecosystems.

H2.1. The influence of entrepreneurial ecosystems on the sustainable high growth of enterprises is moderated by enterprise characteristics such as age, size, scope of operations, and knowledge intensity of their activities.

H2.2. Prior sustainable high growth of enterprises moderates the impact of entrepreneurial ecosystems on future sustainable high growth of these enterprises.

Models 3a–3f showed that resource-based factors (firm age and industry knowledge intensity) are moderators of certain EE dimensions, specifically affecting the human resource competency dimension, the knowledge development and research activity dimension, and the aggregate EE index. Based on these results, Hypothesis H2.1 has been confirmed.

Models 4a–4c confirm Hypothesis H2.2 that EEs, both at the level of dimensions (human resource competency dimension and knowledge development and research activity dimension) and at the aggregate level, have a greater impact on enterprises that recorded prior sustainable high growth. This indicates that enterprises with previous SHG have accumulated resources that increase their chances of achieving SHG in the following period.

Since both H2.1 and H2.2 were confirmed, H2 can also be considered verified. Heterogeneity of enterprises in terms of prior SHG is a moderator of the impact of EE in the human resource competency dimension, the knowledge development and research activity dimension, and the aggregate EE index.

H3. The impact of entrepreneurial ecosystems on the sustainable high growth of enterprises is moderated by spatial interactions between proximate ecosystems.

The results of Models 5a–5c provide a basis for positive verification of H3. The stronger the spatial interactions, the greater the impact of EE in the human resource competency dimension, the knowledge development and research activity dimension, and as an aggregate EE index. This means that in clusters of EE with high values of these indicators, enterprises have a higher chance of achieving sustainable high growth. The auxiliary Moran's I index, calculated at 0.11, also confirms a weak positive spatial autocorrelation. Table 4.3 presents a summary of the model results and hypothesis verification, as well as information about the variables included in these models.

Discussion of modeling results

The results obtained in this monograph are analyzed below in the context of the existing literature. Reference is also made to the diagnostic characteristics of the models used in the study.

Overall EE and its structural characteristics

The conducted research confirms the positive impact of EEs on SHG, which is consistent with most previous studies (Davari & Najmabadi, 2018; Koroleva, 2022; Stam & Van De Ven, 2021). Models 1 and 2, used to verify H1, showed that the structure of EE is useful in explaining the phenomenon of sustainable entrepreneurship. At the aggregate level, where the overall impact of EE on the share of SHG enterprises was analyzed, the R^2 was 0.5766. Similarly, high coefficients of determination for the impact of EE on SHG were obtained in Iran (0.58) (Davari & Najmabadi, 2018), the Netherlands (0.437) (Stam & Van De Ven, 2021, p. 202), and Indonesia (0.478) (Lubis et al., 2023).

Some EE dimensions show significant regional variation in their impact on SHG (Vedula & Fitza, 2019). However, they differ in their structural differentiating power, and some, such as internal market dynamics, have no differentiating power at all (Coduras et al., 2018). In the present study, it was found that in the two most developed ecosystems (Mazowieckie and Małopolskie

Table 4.3 Summary of model results

Level of analysis	*Model*	*Identified determinants*	*Hypothesis verification*
Specific dimensions	Model 1	Age of the enterprise, industry knowledge intensity, prior sustainable high growth, spatial interactions, human resource competence dimension, knowledge and research activity development dimension, structural affiliation.	H1. Sustainable high growth of enterprises depends on the structural characteristics of entrepreneurial ecosystems – **verified positively**.
Aggregated entrepreneurship ecosystem	Model 2	Age of the enterprise, industry knowledge intensity, prior sustainable high growth, spatial interactions, aggregated EE index, structural affiliation.	
Aggregated entrepreneurship ecosystem	Model 3a, 3d	Age of the enterprise, industry knowledge intensity, sustainable high growth, spatial interactions, the aggregated EE index, structural affiliation, interactions between enterprise age and industry knowledge intensity, and the aggregated EE.	H2.1. The influence of entrepreneurial ecosystems on the sustainable high growth of enterprises is moderated by enterprise characteristics such as age, size, scope of operations, and knowledge intensity of their activities – **verified positively**.
Specific dimensions	Model 3b, 3c, 3e, 3f	The age of the enterprise, industry knowledge intensity, prior sustainable high growth, spatial interactions, the dimension of human resource competencies, the dimension of knowledge development and research activity, structural affiliation, interactions between the age of enterprises and the industry knowledge intensity, as well as the competencies of human resources and the dimension of knowledge development and research activity.	

(*Continued*)

Table 4.3 (Continued)

Level of analysis	*Model*	*Identified determinants*	*Hypothesis verification*
Aggregated entrepreneurship ecosystem	Model 4a	Age of the enterprise, industry knowledge intensity, prior sustainable high growth, spatial interactions, aggregated EE index, structural affiliation, interactions between prior sustainable high growth and the aggregated EE.	H2.2 Prior sustainable high growth of enterprises moderates the impact of entrepreneurial ecosystems on future sustainable high growth of these enterprises – **verified positively**.
Specific dimensions	Model 4b, 4c	Age of the enterprise, industry knowledge intensity, prior sustainable high growth, spatial interactions, human resource competencies, the dimension of knowledge development and research activity, structural affiliation, and interactions between prior sustainable high growth and human resource competencies as well as the dimension of knowledge development and research activity.	
Aggregated entrepreneurship ecosystem	Model 5a	The age of the enterprise, industry knowledge intensity, prior sustainable high growth, spatial interactions, the aggregated EE index, structural affiliation, interactions between spatial interactions and the aggregated EE.	H3 The impact of entrepreneurial ecosystems on the sustainable high growth of enterprises is moderated by spatial interactions between proximate ecosystems – **verified positively**.
Specific dimensions	Model 5b, 5c	Age of the enterprise, industry knowledge intensity, prior sustainable high growth, spatial interactions, the human resource competence dimension, the knowledge and research activity development dimension, structural affiliation, interactions between spatial interactions and the dimensions of human resource competence as well as knowledge and research activity development.	

Source: Own research.

regions), the probability of achieving sustainable high growth is lower than what would be expected based on EE conditions (Models 1 and 2). A similar gap between theoretical EE outcomes and local conditions was observed in Bengaluru, India (Muthuraman& Mungila Hillemane, 2020).

It should be noted that the relationships between dimensions, and within them, are complex, and studies often involve significant simplifications. In particular, the use of equal weights in models poses a challenge (Komlósi et al., 2024). This study addressed this issue by applying a quasi-optimal weighting system, which determines the influence of each variable on SHG within each dimension. This approach also resolved the problem of nonlinearity within each dimension, which is an inherent characteristic of EE (Roundy et al., 2018). Such nonlinear relationships and complex interactions between the individual EE dimensions may suggest that structural diversity affects the probability of sustainable high enterprise growth.

Cluster 1 was characterized by better values in all dimensions except the institutional quality dimension. Notably, it had high outlier values for the physical infrastructure dimension and the human resource competency dimension, which may indicate a bottleneck effect (Acs et al., 2017; Autio & Levie, 2017; Wachira, 2022). As a result, enterprises may not be able to fully exploit the potential of these dimensions because other, less developed dimensions constrain potential growth. This may also explain why the significance of clusters representing EE structure, both at the dimension level and for the aggregate index, may suggest an indirect influence of statistically insignificant dimensions on SHG.

Ruland (2013) found in his research that having a headquarters in the largest metropolises is costly, which may reduce financial performance. This could be another explanation for the significance of the variable derived from cluster analysis. Cluster 1 includes the Mazowieckie and Małopolskie regions, which contain Poland's largest cities, Warsaw and Kraków, and are likely the most expensive. Considering that financial indicators are included in the SHG index, this may negatively affect SHG. The variable representing the cluster may also convey information about the costs within a given EE.

EE dimensions can also be partially substitutive, and a low level of technical knowledge may be compensated by a collectivist culture and easy access to financing (Vedula & Fitza, 2019). In studies on EEs, different combinations of dimensions are used; however, their number can be reduced to 2–5 without a significant drop in explained variance (Gancarczyk & Konopa, 2021; Villegas-Mateos & Vázquez-Maguirre, 2020).

The performance of EEs can be similar for different configurations of EE dimensions (Xie et al., 2021). Even in Europe, not all EE dimensions are necessary for high enterprise performance. The diversity of EE requires adapting regional policies to specific regions (Feldman et al., 2019). It is also noted that in almost all studies, institutional data are used, and the level of EE actors themselves is often overlooked, even though it appears to be crucial for ecosystem outcomes (Komlósi et al., 2024). EE actors themselves also consider their influence on EE outcomes to be significant (Muñoz et al., 2022).

There are also views that EEs should be considered holistically, even though certain dimensions seem to have a key impact on EE outcomes (Lehmann, 2020; Luo & Lu, 2024). Acs additionally notes that the development level of EE is strongly correlated with economic growth (Acs et al., 2018). In this study, the correlation between the synthetic EE index and regional GDP within the EE was 0.86. In none of the models was the regional GDP variable statistically significant. This indicates that a development indicator measured by a single monetary variable has lower explanatory power for SHG than the quality of the EE itself. The aggregate EE index encompasses many more characteristics that are important for business activity.

Human capital competence dimension

The research showed that the human capital competence dimension positively affects the SHG of enterprises (Model 1). A similar impact of human capital competence on firm performance was observed in Iran (Davari & Najmabadi, 2018). Human capital proved to be a necessary condition for firm outcomes in the form of innovation in studies conducted in Brazil (Cherubini Alves et al., 2021). Similarly, universities were found to be a necessary condition for high enterprise innovativeness (Cherubini Alves et al., 2021). Research also demonstrated a positive impact of universities and skilled personnel, although this effect shows strong regional variation (Vedula & Fitza, 2019).

High workforce competence, including higher education and continuous learning, positively influenced SHG entrepreneurship. The proportion of doctoral students has no practical significance (due to its low weight – 0.047) for sustainable high growth. This indicates that doctoral students contribute minimally to sales growth or cost reduction in enterprises. This may be due to the small number of doctoral students per enterprise, meaning only a few firms can benefit from their knowledge. Another explanation is their theoretical education, which is of limited practical use to entrepreneurs. In Western countries, it has long been noted that doctoral education should equip students with skills useful outside academia. The close collaboration between universities and industry, implemented in Poland through industrial doctorates, is beneficial for developing such skills (Kosieradzka & Zawiła-Niedźwiecki, 2021; Sokołowski & Sobiech, 2022; Tavares et al., 2020).

A broader societal education has significantly greater importance, reflected in high secondary school graduation rates and the proportion of people with higher education. The share of individuals engaged in continuing education is also important. All enterprises benefit from a well-educated society, which can be seen as a competitive advantage for firms and EEs (Hatch & Dyer, 2004;

Schuller & Field, 2013; Walberg & Stariha, 1992). University studies help strengthen teamwork skills, stress resilience, and critical thinking (Abuzyarova et al., 2019).

Enterprise success largely depends on employee skills. Studies show that intellectual capital positively impacts financial indicators (Bernthal & Wellins, 2006; Cho et al., 2006; Ghebregiorgis & Karsten, 2007; Riahi-Belkaoui, 2003; Rodríguez-Gulías et al., 2021) and market share (Delaney & Huselid, 1996). When implementing organizational changes or new initiatives, employee training helps generate profits (Barton & Delbridge, 2001). The effectiveness of human capital is positively correlated with return on assets (ROA), and human capital has a greater impact on productivity and sales growth than physical or structural capital (Nurseha et al., 2024). Effective management of human capital plays a significant role in a firm's long-term performance (Brennan & Connell, 2000). Training courses positively affect employee productivity, thereby reducing unit labor costs (Bartel, 1994; Black & Lynch, 1996; Brennan & Connell, 2000). A competent HR department has an indirect impact on profitability, solvency, and financial liquidity (Faems et al., 2005). These effects can accumulate at the regional level, increasing the level of high-quality entrepreneurship in EEs. It is worth noting that the human capital competence dimension and the knowledge development and research dimension are interrelated. A high level of education promotes knowledge dissemination and innovation. Research activity and initiatives promoting knowledge collaboration contribute to raising the overall education level in society.

Knowledge development and research activity

Model 1 demonstrated that the dimension of knowledge development and research activity is significant for the SHG of enterprises. Research confirms the positive impact of the R&D dimension on firm performance, though the effect is modest (Davari & Najmabadi, 2018). The innovation expenditure dimension had a positive influence on sustainable high entrepreneurship across all European macro-regions, but in Central Europe, it was lower than in the Mediterranean and Northwestern macro-regions (Komlósi et al., 2024). Technology absorption has also been cited as a factor positively affecting sustainable high entrepreneurship, although this relationship does not hold in all regions studied (Komlósi et al., 2024). Furthermore, the knowledge dimension was statistically significant for generating sustainable high entrepreneurship in Indonesia (Lubis et al., 2023).

However, some studies have found the opposite relationship. For example, Yan and Guan (2019) reported a negative impact of R&D knowledge transfers on entrepreneurial activity. Higher R&D expenditures lead, over a multi-year horizon, to increased enterprise profits (Chen et al., 2005; Hartmann, 2003; Hartmann et al., 2006). Especially firms capable of promoting their products at a large scale gain significant returns from strong R&D investment (Das et al., 2009). The translation of R&D spending into profitability is particularly visible for large-scale investments. Small expenditures may even lead to the opposite effect (Krčál, 2014). R&D expenditures positively influence firm profitability measured by ROA, particularly in the IT sector (Dave et al., 2013).

Another aspect of the impact of EEs on SHG is collaboration in innovation. Research shows that network activities affect sales value. Diversification within collaboration networks influences sales volume. This effect varies with firm size (Parida et al., 2016). For small enterprises, increased network diversity tends to reduce sales, mainly due to the challenges of managing the network. However, as firm size grows, the relationship between network diversification and sales takes a U-shaped form, and the effect turns positive (Parida et al., 2016). Small firms are not well-suited to operate in highly heterogeneous networks, primarily due to transaction costs and limited resources (Goerzen & Beamish, 2005). In the research sample, there were predominantly small, medium, and large firms, which outnumbered micro-enterprises. Therefore, a high share of enterprises collaborating within networks can positively affect sales, increasing the likelihood of achieving SHG.

Firms that introduced more than one type of innovation in the last five years have a higher chance of achieving high sales, order volumes, and export levels (Nunes et al., 2019). Firms engaged in innovation collaboration (both formal and informal) are more likely to introduce innovations, which indirectly contribute to strong future economic performance (Nunes et al., 2019).

Institutional quality

The research results indicate that the institution quality dimension does not have an impact on the SHG of enterprises. Findings from other studies are inconclusive. Some research confirms a positive influence of institutional factors on sustainable high entrepreneurship (Yan & Guan, 2019). For example, studies conducted in Indonesia showed that network collaboration positively affects sustainable high entrepreneurship (Lubis et al., 2023). Other studies indicate that cultural factors, as well as legal regulations and participation in their creation, positively influence the number of newly established enterprises (Davari & Najmabadi, 2018).

However, not all analyses show a positive relationship. According to research conducted in São Paulo, culture can support firm innovativeness, but this effect is not present in all entrepreneurial ecosystems (Cherubini Alves et al., 2021). Studies by Aliyari (2024) show that institutional factors, except for legal ones, do not significantly affect sustainable high entrepreneurship. Previous research involving the monograph author also did not confirm a link between institutional factors and the financial performance of high-growth firms (Gancarczyk & Konopa, 2021). Crime seems to be no longer a sufficiently serious problem to hinder entrepreneurship today.

Collaboration within clusters has proven to be an insufficient condition for SHG, although some studies suggest otherwise. Even though clusters exist in Poland and policies have been implemented to support their development, large firms are the preferred participants in these initiatives. The criteria for selecting participants for the National Key Clusters program include high sales revenue, employment, activities supporting the circular economy, low-emission economy, engagement with the local community, and quality certifications. Additional points are awarded for providing digital sales and procurement platforms (Haberla, 2016). According to the findings of this monograph, state policies aimed at promoting SHG should focus less on the aforementioned criteria and cluster collaboration per se, and more on collaboration aimed at knowledge development and research activities.

Physical infrastructure

Model 1 did not show an impact of physical infrastructure on the SHG entrepreneurship. This conclusion does not align with most studies, where infrastructure was considered as a separate dimension. Research conducted by other scholars indicates that a well-developed infrastructure had a positive effect on firm performance and the proportion of the population engaged in entrepreneurial activity (Davari & Najmabadi, 2018; Yan & Guan, 2019). A well-developed infrastructure dimension of the EE supported innovation in the EE, but it was not a necessary condition for its existence (Cherubini Alves et al., 2021). In Peru, a relationship was also found between the quality of physical infrastructure and SHG entrepreneurship generated by EE (Charles & Zegarra, 2014).

The lack of impact of physical infrastructure on SHG can be partly explained by the construction of the index describing it, which includes financial indicators. While the availability of road infrastructure can be directly linked to enterprise costs, the availability of buildings constructed for specific types of activities or the length of telecommunication lines does not directly affect costs. What matters are the costs of utilizing these infrastructures, which are not considered in the given dimension. Moreover, the number of airline passengers reflects mobility and population flows within the EE but does not necessarily correspond to cargo flight traffic, making it unclear to what extent this variable affects transportation costs.

Access to finance

The financing dimension does not influence SHG in Model 1. In contrast, most previous studies found financing to be important for SHG entrepreneurship (Davari & Najmabadi, 2018; Yan & Guan, 2019). Research shows that financing plays a varied role in shaping firm innovativeness. In some EEs, it is a necessary condition for achieving innovation; in others, its absence was crucial for good performance; and in yet others, it had a positive effect but was not a necessary condition for innovation to occur (Cherubini Alves et al., 2021).

According to Komlósi et al. (2024), analyses of EE dimension configurations leading to SHG entrepreneurship indicate regional variation in the role of financing. In the Northern European macroregion and Central European countries, financing has a highly heterogeneous impact on SHG. In the Mediterranean region, it was a necessary condition for SHG to occur (Komlósi et al., 2024). National-level analyses confirm that the impact of the financing dimension on growth is greater in highly developed countries (Gomes et al., 2023).

In interviews with entrepreneurs, the financing dimension based on government financial support rarely appeared as important from the perspective of startups (Suresh & Ramraj, 2012). An explanation for why the financing dimension proved insignificant in the study may lie in the nature of sustainable high-growth firms. Since these firms are oriented toward high sales revenue, they must take risky decisions. Companies that finance their activities from external sources may exhibit a higher risk aversion.

Digital economy

The monograph's research did not confirm a statistically significant impact of the digital economy dimension on SHG. Studies on the impact of this dimension on sustainable entrepreneurship are scarce. Xie (2021) showed that access to good internet infrastructure is one of the most important factors in the digital entrepreneurship era, affecting both quantitative and qualitative outcomes of EE.

In Poland, the digital economy is relatively underdeveloped in terms of both the digitalization of the economy and society compared to the EU average (Stavytskyy et al., 2019). The digitalization gap, compared with more developed countries, is particularly visible in the impact of the ICT sector on society and the adoption of digital systems. This situation is attributed to poor promotion of digital solutions among society and businesses, as well as low levels of digital skills (Moroz, 2017; Śledziewska & Włoch, 2015; Weresa, 2017).

The monograph's research did not show a relationship between the digital economy index in EE and the SHG of firms. Polish enterprises demonstrate higher chances of sustainable high growth in regions characterized by a high level of knowledge development and R&D expenditures. However, this innovation does not concern the latest digitalization solutions. Another reason for the insignificance of this dimension may be the inclusion of urbanization in the study, which research shows strongly influences technology and knowledge diffusion (Bohlin et al., 2010; Lechman, 2018).

Moderating effects of resource factors and spatial interactions on SHG

Resource-based factors

In this study, resource factors are treated as moderators of the impact of EE on SHG; they also exhibit a statistically significant effect on SHG (model 1 and 2). Among the resource-related variables, the scope of operations does not have a statistically significant impact on SHG. A broad scope in knowledge-intensive activities is much more important. The age of the enterprise plays a significant role in the chances of achieving SHG – younger firms have better opportunities to adapt to market conditions, confirming evolutionary growth theories.

A statistically significant relationship was also found for the impact of spatial interactions on SHG, which would confirm Tobler's first law, stating that spatial proximity influences the similarity of objects. Firm size had no impact on sustainable growth. However, enterprises that experienced sustainable high growth in the previous year had a higher chance of achieving SHG in the following period, confirming Penrose's resource-based theory of the firm. The model results clearly showed a relationship between SHG and the level of local urbanization, included as a control variable. In cities, especially large ones, firms benefit from a well-educated workforce, and also from the high concentration of companies in a small area, which facilitates network connections (Ruland, 2013).

The research results demonstrated the existence of interactions between the human capital competence dimension, the knowledge and R&D dimension, and the aggregated EE index with firm age, industry knowledge intensity, prior SHG, and spatial interactions. The moderating effects of resource factors and spatial interactions on the impact of EEs on SHG are visible both for the aggregated EE and its individual dimensions.

The positive impact of EEs decreases with firm age. Similar results were reported by Vedula and Fitza (2019), who concluded that the performance of older firms depends less on EE. Furthermore, the knowledge intensity of activities is a factor moderating the effect of EEs. Other studies showed that the presence of universities in ecosystems moderated several of the firm's resource factors, positively influencing sales volumes achieved (Link & Sarala, 2019).

Other studies have also examined the moderating effect of entrepreneurship types in the Kirzner and Schumpeter framework. For Schumpeterian entrepreneurship, representing a qualitative direction of development, growth is independent of the quality of the ecosystem. In contrast, for Kirznerian entrepreneurship, representing a quantitative approach, high-quality EEs positively influenced firm growth measured by employment (Szerb et al., 2019). If we assume that the scope of activities corresponds to Kirznerian entrepreneurship, and knowledge intensity to the qualitative Schumpeterian approach, this study shows the opposite relationship: firms engaged in knowledge-intensive activities are more influenced by EE.

There are also other studies analyzing the effects of interactions between resource-based variables and EEs. A method similar to that applied in this monograph was used to examine differences in the impact of EEs on entrepreneurial activity by gender (Hechavarría & Ingram, 2019). However, it was not possible to obtain gender data for the entrepreneurs in the present study.

Prior SHG strengthened the positive effect of EEs, indicating better market orientation and opportunity exploitation by firms that had already achieved SHG, and at the same time confirming resource-based and evolutionary theories. The monograph also confirmed the moderating effect of spatial interactions on EE. Similar results regarding the influence of spatial proximity have been reported in other studies. In Sweden, the effect of knowledge intensity on firm performance was examined. The regional knowledge intensity index was defined to reflect the ratio of skilled personnel to total personnel, including neighboring regions. It was found that high regional knowledge intensity positively influenced sales growth, employment, and labor productivity. This effect was present for the fastest-growing firms, whereas for firms among the 10% slowest-growing, high knowledge density had a negative impact (Grillitsch & Nilsson, 2019). Earlier research by the same authors showed that firms with low internal knowledge resources grow faster in knowledge-intensive regions (Grillitsch & Nilsson, 2017).

A greater impact of EE in regions with high spatial interaction values may indicate the diffusion of know-how conducive to SHG. Raspe and Van Oort (2008) also showed that in regions with a high share of innovative firms and in regions with high R&D intensity, firms achieve higher growth rates (Raspe & Van Oort, 2008). Analysis of changes in firm shares between 2019–2020 and 2021–2022 indicates no spatial differences in the dynamics of SHG shares in EE, and observed changes appear random and statistically insignificant.

The heterogeneous impact of EE factors, resource-based factors, and spatial interactions on SHG may also be reflected in the distributions of logistic regression parameters, which, despite a large number of iterations, have difficulty forming a normal distribution. This may indicate the complex influence of these factors on SHG.

In summary, to verify H2 and H3, a study of the marginal effects of resource-based factors and spatial interactions was conducted. In the case of resource-based factors, this approach helped identify which firm characteristics determine the strength of EE's impact on SHG. It allowed identifying the main beneficiary of EEs: a young firm engaged in a large number of knowledge-intensive activities, located in a region with high spatial interactions, that is, surrounded by EEs with a high share of SHG.

Diagnostic features of the models

Due to the rarity of SHG among firms, a large sample was necessary to demonstrate it. The impact of EEs on the SHG of individual firms is not strong. The

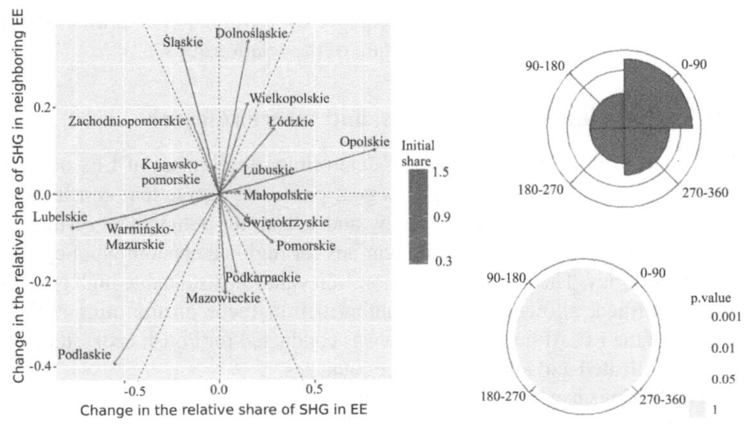

Figure 4.5 Directional LISA

effects of EE are more visible at the aggregate level, which can be explained by interactions between elements of the EE and a combination of resource and spatial factors. The model for aggregated data has a high R^2 value (0.5766) and can serve as an approximation of the quality of panel logistic regression models. The results of EE's impact on SHG can be successfully applied in regional planning, both for diagnosing regional weaknesses and for evaluating the effectiveness of regional policy in terms of entrepreneurship. It is worth noting that EEs in Poland are still in the early stages of development, and their role is likely to increase.

The McFadden pseudo R^2 was 0.030 for model 1 (for the non-panel version of model 1, it was 0.0623), and 0.031 for model 2, which is relatively low. Low pseudo R^2 values are standard when modeling weak relationships. In logistic regression studies, a pseudo R^2 of 0.2 is considered good and roughly corresponds to an R^2 of 0.7–0.9 in linear regression (Ben-Akiva & Lerman, 1985; Louviere, 2000). In preference modeling, low McFadden pseudo R^2 values are often reported (Khan et al., 2020; Naidoo & Adamowicz, 2005; Shen & Saijo, 2009). Higher pseudo R^2 values in models 2 and 4 confirm the importance of the structural characteristics of EE for SHG.

For comparison, models with equal weights were also estimated, yielding results quite similar to the models used in the study. The results for equal-weight models are not presented in this monograph because quasi-optimal weighted models had better Akaike Information Criterion values. The nonlinear correlation coefficient ξ reached 0.2 for quasi-optimal weights and 0.14 for equal weights, indicating that after weighting, the variables retained their linear nature. The Monte Carlo-generated weights remained stable when averaging the top 10% of models according to AIC. Bayesian analyses show that the model does not achieve convergence even with 200,000 draws, which may indicate a strongly nonlinear nature of the relationships.

4.5 Contribution, limitations, and future research

The monograph achieved its goal of determining the impact of EEs on sustainable firm growth. Achieving this goal produced results that constitute a contribution to science, methodology, and economic policy. The results of this monograph have practical implications for regional economic policy and industrial policy. The key EE dimensions relevant for sustainable high growth were identified, allowing regional authorities to focus on the most critical aspects of the EE. Although the study was conducted for Polish ecosystems, it can be replicated and adapted to other countries.

The findings can have a significant impact on regional policy and planned development strategies. Knowledge of which factors and to what extent influence SHG can guide policymakers toward specific actions aimed at developing EEs. Government and local programs supporting entrepreneurship are important for the creation of new firms (Hechavarría & Ingram, 2019). The SHG index includes employment growth, so improving EE conditions should contribute to job creation and thus reduce unemployment.

Establishing the weights of factors within each dimension allows for identifying the key elements important for SHG and focusing on them in the design of regional programs. Confirmation of the impact of EE on SHG provides justification for creating regional competitiveness rankings, which in turn partially influence firms' location decisions. Based on quasi-optimal weights, it is possible to revalidate indicators used in such rankings or to create a completely new ranking measuring the ability of EE to generate SHG.

Contribution to science

The monograph contributes to science by filling a research gap regarding the impact of EE on SHG. It demonstrates that the structural characteristics of EE influence SHG of firms. It also shows that resource factors and spatial interactions modify the impact of EE dimensions, making the overall effect complex. The work contributes to two research streams: studies on SHG and firm size dynamics, and research on EEs. The monograph represents a significant contribution to the current stream of research on EEs and their effect in the form of sustainable high entrepreneurship.

First, the study conceptualized SHG based on a comprehensive, narrative review of the literature on firm growth and EEs. In recent years, the literature on EE has debated what should be considered the outcome of their operation, and in particular, how to understand sustainable high entrepreneurship as a proposed effect of EE (Kansheba, 2020; Koroleva, 2022; Stam & Van De

Ven, 2021). Measures such as rapid revenue growth or market valuation (e.g., "unicorns") do not reflect societal usefulness. Moreover, unicorns are such a rare phenomenon that they are unsuitable for quantitative measurement of EE outcomes (Coeurderoy & Murray, 2008; Poon et al., 2023; Torres & Godinho, 2022; Venâncio et al., 2023).

Current research equates EE outcomes with productive entrepreneurship, typically measured as rapid firm growth, most often via revenue dynamics (Lopez-Garcia & Puente, 2012). This approach neglects the sustainable growth aspect, which combines economic performance (financial health, and profitability) with societal value in the form of employment creation. The SHG concept integrates ideas of rapid growth and sustainability, derived from profitability and employment, which are crucial for firm survival, development, and social relevance. Sustainable, highly growing firms are a very important category in the economy. They are more likely to expand than other firms, less vulnerable to failure, and have a higher probability of expanding into foreign markets. By seeking growth opportunities, they create and proliferate their niche, with other firms acting as imitators.

Second, in line with these conceptual frameworks, the monograph developed a method for measuring SHG and EEs, as well as the relationships between them, making a methodological contribution. An original SHG index was constructed, and the study examined if and how it is influenced by the aggregated EE, its individual dimensions, and resource-based factors of firms. Interactions between EEs, their dimensions, and resource factors were also investigated, which likely constitutes the first study of this kind in the field of EE and firm growth research. The SHG index included sales dynamics, ROE, and solvency and current liquidity ratios. High values of these indicators support resilience to failure. Firm growth should generate benefits for both society and the enterprise, which is why employment growth was included as a social aspect of growth (Baumol, 1996; Minniti et al., 2024).

The monograph contributes to science by developing an index that encompasses aspects important to society and the firms themselves. The proposed EE index is also one of the few composite measures of sustainable high entrepreneurship, as most studies rely on a single-variable measurement (Leendertse et al., 2022). The SHG concept and its measurement can serve as a basis for assessing the effectiveness of EEs. There is a positive relationship between the quality of the overall ecosystem and the probability of achieving SHG, as well as between the share of sustainable highly growing firms within ecosystems, confirming the usefulness of the SHG concept as a measure of EE effectiveness.

A novel set of research techniques was employed in this study. Among them was a nonlinear weighting system used to determine the internal structure of the dimensions of EEs. The need for using weights has been highlighted in numerous previous studies. This approach allowed for determining the informational strength of variables within each dimension, which made it possible to establish their relative importance and thus their internal structure within the EE.

Furthermore, to demonstrate the impact of the structural diversity of EEs on sustainable high entrepreneurship, panel regression on microdata was used. This represents a novelty compared to previous studies, which relied on aggregated data. The use of microdata allowed for identifying interactions between firm resource factors and EEs, which cannot be established with aggregated data. The application of microdata positions this study as original in both Polish and international literature.

The study presented in this monograph is the first quantitative study using microdata to examine the comprehensive impact of EEs on firms. Previous few quantitative studies focused on aggregated data at regional or national levels (Gancarczyk & Konopa, 2021; Torres & Godinho, 2022). Such aggregation does not allow for consideration of firm-level resource factors. The use of microdata enabled a reliable confirmation of the influence of EE on SHG. Supporting analyses at the aggregated level also confirmed this effect. The strong influence of EEs on the share of productively growing firms among all firms is comparable to other studies on EE performance outcomes (Koroleva, 2022; Stam & Van De Ven, 2021).The use of microdata also allowed for identifying which factors influence company SHG. The obtained results partially confirm the findings of previous researchers; however, full comparability is limited because most studies focus on high-growth firms, whereas the results presented in this monograph are also novel conceptually and methodologically, proposing the idea of SHG.

A strength of the study is the sample selection, which is representative in terms of both the geographical location of firms and industry sectors. Many studies on firm growth focus on a small number of highly selected firms or specific sectors, which means that their results reflect only a small fragment of business activity (Beekman & Robinson, 2004; Delmar et al., 2003; Moghaddam et al., 2019). The use of panel data also addresses the insufficient consideration of the time dimension in EE research (Brown & Mason, 2017; Roundy et al., 2018; Trabskaja & Mets, 2019).

Research limitations

The first limitation is the restriction of the study period to 2018–2022, due to the lack of access to firm financial data for 2015 and earlier. Expanding the time frame would increase the diversity of regional data, allowing for a more accurate assessment of its impact on SHG. As companies are now required to submit electronic financial reports, it will be possible to extend future studies to subsequent years.

The second limitation is the small number of firms with financial data in CEIDG. Most enterprises registered in CEIDG are not required to maintain full accounting records, so financial data are not available. Since such firms constitute the majority of businesses in Poland, the results presented do not reflect the impact of EE on the most representative group. However, many micro-enterprises are self-employed individuals, for whom owning a company replaces full-time employment (Buchelt et al., 2016; Mockałło & Barańska, 2022; Puzio-Wacławik, 2013; Szepelska, 2013). Such individuals are generally not interested in firm growth.

The study does not include information on inter-company links, as such data could not be obtained. However, the vast majority of firms are independent enterprises, and the large sample size used in this study further reduces the risk of bias.

Another limitation is the use of PKD codes only for 2024, which prevents a precise assessment of the impact of scope of activity and knowledge intensity of sectors on SHG as variables with a longer time horizon would allow. During the study period, the COVID-19 pandemic and the war in Ukraine occurred, potentially affecting firms' financial results and sales, and thus the study outcomes. To eliminate this effect, the study period could have been limited to 2018–2019, which would have significantly reduced the availability and diversity of EE data. As noted earlier, the data do not show a pandemic impact, but due to their specific nature, no formal tests were conducted. Nevertheless, the benefits of using the maximum available range outweigh the potential bias from exogenous shocks. The absence of lagged variables is another limitation. The study does not consider the delayed response of firms and adaptation processes to changes in EE conditions. Using EE indicators lagged by one year or averaged over the past two years might yield better results.

Bibliography

Abuzyarova, D., Belousova, V., Krayushkina, Z., Lonshcikova, Y., Nikiforova, E., & Chichkanov, N. (2019). The role of human capital in science. *Technology and Innovation. Форсайт, 13*(2 (eng)), 107–119.

Acs, Z. J., Estrin, S., Mickiewicz, T., & Szerb, L. (2018). Entrepreneurship, institutional economics, and economic growth: An ecosystem perspective. *Small Business Economics, 51*(2), 501–514. https://doi.org/10.1007/s11187-018-0013-9

Acs, Z. J., Stam, E., Audretsch, D. B., & O'Connor, A. (2017). The lineages of the entrepreneurial ecosystem approach. *Small Business Economics, 49*(1), 1–10. https://doi.org/10.1007/s11187-017-9864-8

Aliyari, M. (2024). The impact of entrepreneurship ecosystem on the success of start-ups. *International Journal of Applied Research in Management, Economics and Accounting, 1*(3), 16–23.

Autio, E., & Levie, J. (2017). Management of entrepreneurial ecosystems. In G. Ahmetoglu, T. Chamorro-Premuzic, B. Klinger, & T. Karcisky (Eds.), *The Wiley handbook of entrepreneurship* (1st ed., pp. 423–449). Wiley. https://doi.org/10.1002/9781118970812.ch19

Bartel, A. P. (1994). Productivity gains from the implementation of employee training programs. *Industrial Relations: A Journal of Economy and Society, 33*(4), 411–425. https://doi.org/10.1111/j.1468-232X.1994.tb00349.x

Barton, H., & Delbridge, R. (2001). Development in the learning factory: Training human capital. *Journal of European Industrial Training*, *25*(9), 465–472.

Baumol, W. J. (1996). Entrepreneurship: Productive, unproductive, and destructive. *Journal of Business Venturing*, *11*(1), 3–22.

Beekman, A. V., & Robinson, R. B. (2004). Supplier partnerships and the small, high-growth firm: Selecting for success. *Journal of Small Business Management*, *42*(1), 59–77. https://doi.org/10.1111/j.1540-627X.2004.00097.x

Ben-Akiva, M. E., & Lerman, S. R. (1985). *Discrete choice analysis: Theory and application to travel demand* (Vol. 9). MIT Press. https://books.google.com/books?hl=pl&lr=&id=oLC6ZYPs9UoC&oi=fnd&pg=PR14&dq=ben-akiva+lerman+1985&ots=nPcqnYelKj&sig=3MxGi3LeB58OnC1kP1teJ2fVKu8

Bernthal, P., & Wellins, R. (2006). Trends in leader development and succession. *Human Resource Planning*, *29*(2), 31–40. https://search.ebscohost.com/login.aspx?direct=true&profile=ehost&scope=site&authtype=crawler&jrnl=01998986&AN=22299859&h=Q8m9atMR53y1M2rGdpm1qLyGWSpDv0dJVt81uS7FJ2TiAAuqi43Iogyy%2Bc%2B7nGfnzooZ6UraPumLyften5u%2BeA%3D%3D&crl=c

Black, S. E., & Lynch, L. M. (1996). Human-capital investments and productivity. *The American Economic Review*, *86*(2), 263–267.

Bohlin, A., Gruber, H., & Koutroumpis, P. (2010). Diffusion of new technology generations in mobile communications. *Information Economics and Policy*, *22*(1), 51–60.

Brennan, N., & Connell, B. (2000). Intellectual capital: Current issues and policy implications. *Journal of Intellectual Capital*, *1*(3), 206–240.

Brown, R., & Mason, C. (2017). Looking inside the spiky bits: A critical review and conceptualisation of entrepreneurial ecosystems. *Small Business Economics*, *49*(1), 11–30. https://doi.org/10.1007/s11187-017-9865-7

Buchelt, B. I., Pauli, U., & Pocztowski, A. (2016). *Samozatrudnienie jako forma aktywności zawodowej sprzyjająca ograniczaniu bezrobocia wśród osób młodych w Polsce*, ACTA UNIVERSITATIS LODZIENSIS, FOLIA OECONOMICA 4 (323), 37–52. https://dspace.uni.lodz.pl/handle/11089/21212

Charles, V., & Zegarra, L. F. (2014). Measuring regional competitiveness through data envelopment analysis: A Peruvian case. *Expert Systems with Applications*, *41*(11), 5371–5381.

Chen, M.-C., Cheng, S.-J., & Hwang, Y. (2005). An empirical investigation of the relationship between intellectual capital and firms' market value and financial performance. *Journal of Intellectual Capital*, *6*(2), 159–176.

Cherubini Alves, A., Fischer, B. B., & Vonortas, N. S. (2021). Ecosystems of entrepreneurship: Configurations and critical dimensions. *The Annals of Regional Science*, *67*(1), 73–106. https://doi.org/10.1007/s00168-020-01041-y

Cho, S., Woods, R. H., Jang, S. S., & Erdem, M. (2006). Measuring the impact of human resource management practices on hospitality firms' performances. *International Journal of Hospitality Management*, *25*(2), 262–277.

Coduras, A., De La Vega, I., & Salman, M. B. (2018). Entrepreneurial ecosystems in Arabic countries: A recent overview. In N. Faghih & M. R. Zali (Eds.), *Entrepreneurship ecosystem in the Middle East and North Africa (MENA)* (pp. 283–302). Springer International Publishing. https://doi.org/10.1007/978-3-319-75913-5_9

Coeurderoy, R., & Murray, G. (2008). Regulatory environments and the location decisions of start-ups: Evidence from the first international market entries of new technology-based firms. *Journal of International Business Studies*, *39*(4), 670–687. https://dial.uclouvain.be/pr/boreal/object/boreal:18068

Das, A., Kumar, V., Kumar, U., & Haldar, R. (2009). Impact of R&D expenditure on financial performance: A study of Canadian IT firms. Carleton University: Ottawa, ON.

Davari, A., & Najmabadi, A. D. (2018). Entrepreneurial ecosystem and performance in Iran. In N. Faghih & M. R. Zali (Eds.), *Entrepreneurship ecosystem in the Middle East and North Africa (MENA)* (pp. 265–282). Springer International Publishing. https://doi.org/10.1007/978-3-319-75913-5_8

Dave, P., Wadhwa, V., Aggarwal, S., & Seetharaman, A. (2013). The impact of research and development on the financial sustainability of information technology (IT) companies listed on the S&P 500 index. *Journal of Sustainable Development*, *6*(11), 122.

Delaney, J. T., & Huselid, M. A. (1996). The impact of human resource management practices on perceptions of organizational performance. *Academy of Management Journal*, *39*(4), 949–969. https://doi.org/10.2307/256718

Delmar, F., Davidsson, P., & Gartner, W. B. (2003). Arriving at the high-growth firm. *Journal of Business Venturing*, *18*(2), 189–216.

Faems, D., Sels, L., De Winne, S., & Maes, J. (2005). The effect of individual HR domains on financial performance: Evidence from Belgian small businesses. *The International Journal of Human Resource Management*, *16*(5), 676–700. https://doi.org/10.1080/09585190500082790

Feldman, M., Siegel, D. S., & Wright, M. (2019). New developments in innovation and entrepreneurial ecosystems. *Industrial and Corporate Change*, *28*(4), 817–826.

Fischer, B. B., Alves, A. C., Vonortas, N. S., & Brown, R. (2024). Foundations of entrepreneurial ecosystems configurations. *The Journal of Technology Transfer*, 51, 199–225, https://doi.org/10.1007/s10961-024-10147-w

Gancarczyk, M., & Konopa, S. (2021). Exploring the governance of entrepreneurial ecosystems for productive high growth. *Foresight and STI Governance*, *15*(4), 9–21.

Ghebregiorgis, F., & Karsten, L. (2007). Human resource management and performance in a developing country: The case of Eritrea. *The International Journal of Human Resource Management*, *18*(2), 321–332. https://doi.org/10.1080/09585190601102547

Goerzen, A., & Beamish, P. W. (2005). The effect of alliance network diversity on multinational enterprise performance. *Strategic Management Journal*, *26*(4), 333–354. https://doi.org/10.1002/smj.447

Gomes, S., Ferreira, J. J., & Lopes, J. M. (2023). Entrepreneurial conditions and economic growth in entrepreneurial ecosystems: Evidence from OECD countries. *The International Journal of Entrepreneurship and Innovation*, *26*(4), 315–333. https://doi.org/10.1177/14657503231156340

Grillitsch, M., & Nilsson, M. (2017). Firm performance in the periphery: On the relation between firm-internal knowledge and local knowledge spillovers. *Regional Studies*, *51*(8), 1219–1231. https://doi.org/10.1080/00343404.2016.1175554

Grillitsch, M., & Nilsson, M. (2019). Knowledge externalities and firm heterogeneity: Effects on high and low growth firms. *Papers in Regional Science*, *98*(1), 93–114. https://doi.org/10.1111/pirs.12342

Haberla, M. (2016). Cluster development strategy in the context of the "Key National Cluster" competition. *Acta Scientiarum Polonorum. Oeconomia*, *15*(4), 75–82. https://agro.icm.edu.pl/agro/element/bwmeta1.element.agro-fd7ccd7e-5253-425b-952b-e21c582975a7

Hartmann, G. C. (2003). Linking R&D spending to revenue growth. *Research-Technology Management*, *46*(1), 39–46. https://doi.org/10.1080/08956308.2003.11671543

Hartmann, G. C., Myers, M. B., & Rosenbloom, R. S. (2006). Planning your firm's R&D investment. *Research-Technology Management*, *49*(2), 25–36. https://doi.org/10.1080/08956308.2006.11657366

Hatch, N. W., & Dyer, J. H. (2004). Human capital and learning as a source of sustainable competitive advantage. *Strategic Management Journal*, *25*(12), 1155–1178. https://doi.org/10.1002/smj.421

Hechavarría, D. M., & Ingram, A. E. (2019). Entrepreneurial ecosystem conditions and gendered national-level entrepreneurial activity: A 14-year panel study of GEM. *Small Business Economics*, *53*(2), 431–458. https://doi.org/10.1007/s11187-018-9994-7

Kansheba, J. M. P. (2020). Small business and entrepreneurship in Africa: The nexus of entrepreneurial ecosystems and productive entrepreneurship. *Small Enterprise Research*, *27*(2), 110–124. https://doi.org/10.1080/13215906.2020.1761869

Khan, S. U., Hayat, S., Xia, X., Liu, G., & Zhao, M. (2020). Improvisation of indigenous environmental benefit transfer and valuation for cleaner environment: Choice experiment across northwest China. *Journal of Cleaner Production*, *274*, 123176.

Komlósi, É., Dejardin, M., Szerb, L., & Páger, B. (2024). Is a balanced entrepreneurial ecosystem essential for success? A configurational analysis of European regional entrepreneurial ecosystems. *The Journal of Technology Transfer*, *50*, 1669–1708. https://doi.org/10.1007/s10961-024-10149-8

Koroleva, E. (2022). FinTech entrepreneurial ecosystems: Exploring the interplay between input and output. *International Journal of Financial Studies*, *10*(4), 92.

Kosieradzka, A., & Zawiła-Niedźwiecki, J. (2021). *Doktoraty wdrożeniowe i eksternistyczne*. https://repo.pw.edu.pl/info/article/WUTc2d2914a025d4e40a21a59a170dd1d10

Krčál, O. (2014). The relationship between profitability, innovation and technology gap: A basic model. *Review of Economic Perspectives*, *14*(3), 215–231. https://doi.org/10.2478/revecp-2014-0011

Lechman, E. (2018). Networks externalities as social phenomenon in the process ICT diffusion. *Economics and Sociology*, *11*(1), 22–43.

Leendertse, J., Schrijvers, M., & Stam, E. (2022). Measure twice, cut once: Entrepreneurial ecosystem metrics. *Research Policy*, *51*(9), 104336.

Lehmann, M. (2020). Global rules for a global market place?-Regulation and supervision of Fintech providers. *Bosten University International Law Journal*, *38*, 118.

Link, A. N., & Sarala, R. M. (2019). Advancing conceptualisation of university entrepreneurial ecosystems: The role of knowledge-intensive entrepreneurial firms. *International Small Business Journal: Researching Entrepreneurship*, *37*(3), 289–310. https://doi.org/10.1177/0266242618821720

Lopez-Garcia, P., & Puente, S. (2012). What makes a high-growth firm? A dynamic probit analysis using Spanish firm-level data. *Small Business Economics*, *39*(4), 1029–1041. https://doi.org/10.1007/s11187-011-9321-z

Louviere, J. J. (2000). *Stated choice methods: Analysis and applications*. Cambridge University Press. https://books.google.com/books?hl=pl&lr=&id=j-KcAgAAQBAJ&oi=fnd&pg=PR9&dq=Stated+Choice+Methods:+Analysis+and+Applications&ots=9PuDl_dpeD&sig=iqMkGr_u2QtaZD29JMrgbqs16ME

Lubis, A. S., Wijaya, C., & Sakapurnama, E. (2023). Analysis of entrepreneurial ecosystem factors on productive entrepreneurship of digital start-ups in Indonesia. *International Journal of Business Ecosystem & Strategy (2687–2293)*, *5*(3), 11–21.

Luo, Y., & Lu, Y. (2024). Boosting hometown entrepreneurship performance: Insights from entrepreneurial ecosystem theory. *Asia Pacific Economic and Management Review*, *1*(5), 89–105.

Minniti, M., Naudé, W., & Stam, E. (Ed. Minniti) (2024). Is productive entrepreneurship getting scarcer? A reflection on the contemporary relevance of Baumol's typology of entrepreneurship. In *Handbook of research on entrepreneurship and conflict* (pp. 18–44). Edward Elgar Publishing. https://www.elgaronline.com/edcollchap/book/9781802206791/book-part-9781802206791-9.xml

Mockałło, Z., & Barańska, P. (2022). Nowe formy pracy–ich charakterystyka oraz związki z dobrostanem osób pracujących. *Bezpieczeństwo Pracy: Nauka i Praktyka, 9*, 10–14.

Moghaddam, K., Aidov, A., DuVal, C., & Azarpanah, S. (Ed. Moghaddam) (2019). High-growth entrepreneurial firm funding: A qualitative study of native-born and immigrant entrepreneurs. In *Entrepreneurial finance* (pp. 75–94). Routledge. https://www.taylorfrancis.com/chapters/edit/10.4324/9781351202152-5/high-growth-entrepreneurial-firm-funding-qualitative-study-native-born-immigrant-entrepreneurs-kaveh-moghaddam-alexandre-aidov-charles-duval-sara-azarpanah

Moroz, M. (2017). The level of development of the digital economy in Poland and selected European Countries: A comparative analysis. *Foundations of Management, 9*(1), 175–190. https://doi.org/10.1515/fman-2017-0014

Muthuraman, H. B., & Mungila Hillemane, B. S. (2020). Entrepreneurial ecosystem for tech start-ups in Bangalore: An exploration of structure and gap. *Journal of Small Business and Enterprise Development, 27*, 1167–1185. https://doi.org/10.1108/JSBED-07-2019-0233

Muñoz, P., Kibler, E., Mandakovic, V., & Amorós, J. E. (2022). Local entrepreneurial ecosystems as configural narratives: A new way of seeing and evaluating antecedents and outcomes. *Research Policy, 51*(9), 104065.

Naidoo, R., & Adamowicz, W. L. (2005). Biodiversity and nature-based tourism at forest reserves in Uganda. *Environment and Development Economics, 10*(2), 159–178.

Nunes, S., Lopes, R., & Fuller-Love, N. (2019). Networking, innovation, and firms' performance: Portugal as illustration. *Journal of the Knowledge Economy, 10*(3), 899–920. https://doi.org/10.1007/s13132-017-0508-7

Nurseha, B. P., Afif, M. N., & Anwar, S. (2024). The effect of human capital efficiency, structural capital efficiency, relational capital efficiency, capital employed efficiency & rate of growth of intellectual capital on financial performance. *The Accounting Journal of Binaniaga, 9*(01), 51–64.

Parida, V., Patel, P. C., Wincent, J., & Kohtamäki, M. (2016). Network partner diversity, network capability, and sales growth in small firms. *Journal of Business Research, 69*(6), 2113–2117.

Poon, T. S.-C., Wu, C.-H., & Liu, M.-C. (2023). Developing entrepreneurial ecosystem: A case of unicorns in China and its innovation policy implications. *Asian Journal of Technology Innovation, 32*(6), 1–17. https://doi.org/10.1080/19761597.2022.2157849

Puzio-Wacławik, B. (2013). Samozatrudnienie jako element systemowego wsparcia rynku pracy w Polsce. *Studia Ekonomiczne, 145*, 197–207.

Raspe, O., & Van Oort, F. (2008). Firm growth and localized knowledge externalities. *Journal of Regional Analysis and Policy, 38*(2), 100–116.

Riahi-Belkaoui, A. (2003). Intellectual capital and firm performance of US multinational firms: A study of the resource-based and stakeholder views. *Journal of Intellectual Capital, 4*(2), 215–226.

Rodríguez-Gulías, M. J., Fernández-López, S., Rodeiro-Pazos, D., & Nogueira-Moreiras, M. Á. (2021). Technological Innovation and Exports: Effects on Firm Growth. In Technological Innovation and International Competitiveness for Business Growth. Edward Elgar Publishing, 17–39. https://doi.org/10.1007/978-3-030-51995-7_2

Roundy, P. T., Bradshaw, M., & Brockman, B. K. (2018). The emergence of entrepreneurial ecosystems: A complex adaptive systems approach. *Journal of Business Research*, *86*, 1–10.

Ruland, W. (2013). Are big city businesses more profitable than other firms? *Managerial Finance*, *39*(11), 1100–1119.

Schuller, T., & Field, J. (Ed. Schuller, T.) (2013). Social Capital, Human Capital and the Learning Society. In *From adult education to the learning society* (pp. 354–365). Routledge. https://api.taylorfrancis.com/content/chapters/edit/download?identifierName=doi&identifierValue=10.4324/9780203015988-25&type=chapterpdf

Shen, J., & Saijo, T. (2009). Does an energy efficiency label alter consumers' purchasing decisions? A latent class approach based on a stated choice experiment in Shanghai. *Journal of Environmental Management*, *90*(11), 3561–3573.

Śledziewska, K., & Włoch, R. (2015). (Un) Digital Poland: The gap in the digital skills of human capital. *Entrenova-Enterprise Research Innovation*, *1*(1), 486–492.

Sokołowski, K., & Sobiech, K. (2022). *Kadry Przyszłości: 5 lat Doktoratów Wdrożeniowych*. Sieć Badawcza Łukasiewicz.

Stam, E., & Van De Ven, A. (2021). Entrepreneurial ecosystem elements. *Small Business Economics*, *56*(2), 809–832. https://doi.org/10.1007/s11187-019-00270-6

Stavytskyy, A., Kharlamova, G., & Stoica, E. A. (2019). The analysis of the digital economy and society index in the EU. *Baltic Journal of European Studies*, *9*(3), 245–261. https://doi.org/10.1515/bjes-2019-0032

Suresh, J., & Ramraj, R. (2012). Entrepreneurial ecosystem: Case study on the influence of environmental factors on entrepreneurial success. *European Journal of Business and Management*, *4*(16), 95–101.

Szepelska, A. (2013). Samozatrudnienie jako forma wspierania rozwoju przedsiębiorczości regionów. *Ekonomia i Prawo. Economics and Law*, *12*(1), 69–80.

Szerb, L., Lafuente, E., Horváth, K., & Páger, B. (2019). The relevance of quantity and quality entrepreneurship for regional performance: The moderating role of the entrepreneurial ecosystem. *Regional Studies*, *53*(9), 1308–1320. https://doi.org/10.1080/00343404.2018.1510481

Tavares, O., Soares, D., & Sin, C. (2020). Industry–university collaboration in industrial doctorates: A trouble-free marriage? *Industry and Higher Education*, *34*(5), 312–320. https://doi.org/10.1177/0950422219900155

Torres, P., & Godinho, P. (2022). Levels of necessity of entrepreneurial ecosystems elements. *Small Business Economics*, *59*(1), 29–45. https://doi.org/10.1007/s11187-021-00515-3

Trabskaja, J., & Mets, T. (2019). Ecosystem as the source of entrepreneurial opportunities. *Форсайт*, *13*(4 (eng)), 10–22.

Vedula, S., & Fitza, M. (2019). Regional recipes: A configurational analysis of the regional entrepreneurial ecosystem for U.S. Venture capital-backed startups. *Strategy Science*, *4*(1), 4–24. https://doi.org/10.1287/stsc.2019.0076

Venâncio, A., Picoto, W., & Pinto, I. (2023). Time-to-unicorn and digital entrepreneurial ecosystems. *Technological Forecasting and Social Change*, *190*, 122425.

Villegas-Mateos, A., & Vázquez-Maguirre, M. (2020). Social entrepreneurial ecosystems: A regional perspective of Mexico. *International Journal of Entrepreneurship*, *24*(1), 1–19.

Wachira, E. W. (2022). Analysis of Austria's entrepreneurial ecosystem based on the Gei approach. *International Journal of Entrepreneurial Knowledge*, *10*(1), 123–136.

Walberg, H. J., & Stariha, W. E. (1992). Productive human capital: Learning, creativity, and eminence. *Creativity Research Journal*, *5*(4), 323–340. https://doi.org/10.1080/10400419209534445

Weresa, M. A. (2017). Innovation, human capital and competitiveness in Central and Eastern Europe with regard to the challenges of a digital economy. In *Condemned to be left behind?*. Edward Elgar Publishing, 81–109.

Xie, Z., Wang, X., Xie, L., & Duan, K. (2021). Entrepreneurial ecosystem and the quality and quantity of regional entrepreneurship: A configurational approach. *Journal of Business Research*, *128*, 499–509.

Yan, Y., & Guan, J. (2019). Entrepreneurial ecosystem, entrepreneurial rate and innovation: The moderating role of internet attention. *International Entrepreneurship and Management Journal*, *15*(2), 625–650. https://doi.org/10.1007/s11365-018-0493-8

Conclusion

This monograph has accomplished the aim to develop conceptual foundations of the relationship between entrepreneurial ecosystems (EEs) and the firm's sustainable high growth (SHG), and to empirically verify whether and how EEs impact SHG. The aim was addressed on theoretical and empirical grounds.

In the theoretical part of the monograph, we adopt the method of narrative literature review. The review covered theoretical literature and empirical studies in the area EEs, firm growth, and determinants of firm growth. In the empirical part, a method of secondary data analysis was employed, based on reliable databases and sources, such as Orbis, Crunchbase, Statistics Poland's Local Data Bank, and Polish public registers of entrepreneurs. Polish regional EEs in the years 2018–2022 were described using six components as complex variables: physical infrastructure, human resource competencies, access to finance, institutional quality, the digital economy, and the development of knowledge and research activity.

We used the firms' microdata from Orbis to reflect SHG as a complex indicator reflecting size dynamics, profitability, and social benefits. The reliance on microdata is unique compared to the existing research, and it raised a sample of more than 43 thousand firms, representative according to regional distribution, size, and industry. Heterogeneity was captured as other firms' characteristics (e.g. age, size, and scope of activity), and SHG in the previous period. The main research methods were panel logistic regression and the analysis of its marginal effects. Additionally, to support the evaluation of results, we applied spectral clustering analysis and Bayesian logistic regression.

This quantitative approach enables generalization and is scarce, given the predominantly qualitative nature of the EE research stream. Although valuable for in-depth exploration of contextual and multi-factor EEs, qualitative studies enable only an analytical generalization, and not a statistical generalization. Our quantitative method has also responded to the challenge of diversity and uniqueness of territorial units, by using a configurational perspective

DOI: 10.4324/9781003739333-6

(Brown & Mawson, 2019; Capozza et al., 2018; González-López & Asheim, 2020; Mason & Brown, 2014).

The unique value and major contribution from our research rests in the explanation of how EEs can contribute to firms' SHG, acknowledging alternative theoretical approaches, such as the resource-based view, and revealing the EE boundaries through spatial interactions, using data from Polish regional ecosystems in the years 2018–2022. Our research provides *theoretical, methodological, and practical contributions.*

Regarding the theoretical contribution, this book proposes a theoretical advancement by conceptualizing the output of EEs as sustainable high-growth entrepreneurship. We also broaden the empirical evidence on how particular EE dimensions contribute to the expected outcomes and identify the key EE components. This study enhances knowledge building through profiling the complex phenomenon of EE in a particular country context (Hassink et al., 2019). A robust sample selection and a large sample of enterprises studied enhance generalization, despite the one-country context.

Moreover, this research acknowledges unique boundaries of ecosystems that do not necessarily follow the administrative units, such as regions (Fischer et al., 2025; Harima & Harima, 2024; Schäfer, 2021). This was achieved by studying spatial interactions between the proximate EEs in producing SHG, which provided a more refined approach to the understanding of the EE scope and impact.

Furthermore, this research also contributes to the theory of firm growth, by expanding the knowledge of external and spatial conditions for sustainable expansion. The monograph explores how an external environment, formed by different types of EE, associates with SHG, and it identifies the configurations of EE dimensions that are the most effective in producing SHG.

Regarding a methodological contribution, a quantitative identification of the EE determinants of SHG represents an original approach in view of existing research, dominated by qualitative case study methodologies (Audretsch et al., 2024; Stam et al., 2025; Torres & Godinho, 2022; Wurth et al., 2022). Moreover, our method provides the opportunities for replication and adaptation to other regions, beyond Poland. In line with the conceptual frameworks, a method for measuring SHG and ecosystems was developed.

Regarding a policy-relevant contribution, the identified EE characteristics and profiles conducive for SHG might serve as a canvas for setting up entrepreneurship and regional strategies and measures for the upgrade of EEs (Brown & Mawson, 2019). Policymakers might consider the EE dimensions relevant for SHG as benchmarks to develop the tailored public measures for other ecosystems (Brown & Mawson, 2019; Candeias & Sarkar, 2024; Colombelli et al., 2019; Wojnicka-Sycz, 2020).

This study responds to the important research gaps. Firstly, it fills the gap in the research on high growth that consists of overlooking the expected outcomes of expansion, that is, economic efficiency, positive financial indicators, and social values (Baumol, 1959; Bolek, 2018; Coad, 2009; Stam & Van De Ven, 2021; Wurth et al., 2022; Zbierowski, 2012). To address this gap, we propose the conceptualization of productive entrepreneurship as SHG of firms.

Second, it addresses the gap in the understanding of whether and how EEs impact SHG entrepreneurship (Stam, 2018; Stam & Van De Ven, 2021; Xie et al., 2021). We have positively verified this impact by testing three research hypotheses in a robust empirical experiment. The research confirmed verified that the structural characteristics of EEs affect SHG of firms. Our fine-grained approach enabled the identification of company heterogeneity and prior growth as moderators of EE-SHG relationships.

Thirdly, we respond to the gap in specifying the foundations and conceptualizing EEs and productive entrepreneurship. Through a thorough literature review, we systematized the theoretical framework and integrated these grounds with the empirical and conceptual state-of-the-art. These theoretical advances further guided our measurement and procedures in the empirical study.

Bibliography

Audretsch, D. B., Rocha, H., Aggarwal, S., & Bramanti, A. (2024). Do entrepreneurial ecosystems foster sustainable development? *International Entrepreneurship and Management Journal*, *20*(1), 1–37. https://doi.org/10.1007/s11365-023-00916-8

Baumol, W. J. (1959). *Business behavior, value and growth*. Macmillan.

Bolek, M. (2018). *Determinanty wzrostu przedsiębiorstw na rynku kapitałowym*. Wydawnictwo Uniwersytetu Łódzkiego. https://www.ceeol.com/search/book-detail?id=685333

Brown, R., & Mawson, S. (2019). Entrepreneurial ecosystems and public policy in action: A critique of the latest industrial policy blockbuster. *Cambridge Journal of Regions, Economy and Society*, *12*(3), 347–368.

Candeias, J. C., & Sarkar, S. (2024). Entrepreneurial ecosystems policy formulation: A conceptual framework. *Academy of Management Perspectives*, *38*(1), 77–105. https://doi.org/10.5465/amp.2022.0047

Capozza, C., Salomone, S., & Somma, E. (2018). Local industrial structure, agglomeration economies and the creation of innovative start-ups: Evidence from the Italian case. *Entrepreneurship & Regional Development*, *30*(7–8), 749–775. https://doi.org/10.1080/08985626.2018.1457087

Coad, A. (Ed. Coad, A.) (2009). The growth of firms: A survey of theories and empirical evidence. In *The growth of firms: A survey of theories and empirical evidence*. Edward Elgar Publishing Ltd.

Colombelli, A., Paolucci, E., & Ughetto, E. (2019). Hierarchical and relational governance and the life cycle of entrepreneurial ecosystems. *Small Business Economics*, *52*(2), 505–521. https://doi.org/10.1007/s11187-017-9957-4

Fischer, B., Guerrero, M., Mayer, H., Meissner, D., Schäfer, S., & Theodoraki, C. (2025). Entrepreneurial ecosystem as a spatially fluid concept: New territorial perspectives on entrepreneurship. *Small Business Economics*. https://doi.org/10.1007/s11187-025-01020-7

González-López, M., & Asheim, B. T. (2020). *Regions and innovation policies in Europe: Learning from the margins*. Edward Elgar Publishing. https://books.google.com/books?hl=pl&lr=&id=EC7eDwAAQBAJ&oi=fnd&pg=PR1&dq=Regions+and+innovation+policies+in+Europe:+Learning+from+the+margins&ots=sutvwM3LjF&sig=jqh895kHRE0JUs_D1StCaftU_xc

Harima, A., & Harima, J. (2024). Unintended dependence creation? The nesting effect of university entrepreneurial ecosystems. *Academy of Management Perspectives*, *38*(4), 534–555. https://doi.org/10.5465/amp.2023.0048

Hassink, R., Isaksen, A., & Trippl, M. (2019). Towards a comprehensive understanding of new regional industrial path development. *Regional Studies*, *53*(11), 1636–1645. https://doi.org/10.1080/00343404.2019.1566704

Mason, C., & Brown, R. (2014). Entrepreneurial ecosystems and growth oriented entrepreneurship. *Final Report to OECD, Paris*, *30*(1), 77–102.

Schäfer, S. (2021). Spatialities of entrepreneurial ecosystems. *Geography Compass*, *15*(9). https://doi.org/10.1111/gec3.12591

Stam, E. (2018). Measuring entrepreneurial ecosystems. In A. O'Connor, E. Stam, F. Sussan, & D. B. Audretsch (Eds.), *Entrepreneurial ecosystems* (Vol. 38, pp. 173–197). Springer International Publishing. https://doi.org/10.1007/978-3-319-63531-6_9

Stam, E., Theodoraki, C., Bosma, N., Chabaud, D., & Guéneau, G. (2025). Opening entrepreneurial ecosystem black boxes. *Small Business Economics*. https://doi.org/10.1007/s11187-025-01037-y

Stam, E., & Van De Ven, A. (2021). Entrepreneurial ecosystem elements. *Small Business Economics*, *56*(2), 809–832. https://doi.org/10.1007/s11187-019-00270-6

Torres, P., & Godinho, P. (2022). Levels of necessity of entrepreneurial ecosystems elements. *Small Business Economics*, *59*(1), 29–45. https://doi.org/10.1007/s11187-021-00515-3

Wojnicka-Sycz, E. (2020). Theory-based evaluation criteria for regional smart specializations and their application in the Podkarpackie voivodeship in Poland. *Regional Studies*, *54*(11), 1612–1625. https://doi.org/10.1080/00343404.2020.1802419

Wurth, B., Stam, E., & Spigel, B. (2022). Toward an entrepreneurial ecosystem research program. *Entrepreneurship Theory and Practice*, *46*(3), 729–778. https://doi.org/10.1177/1042258721998948

Xie, Z., Wang, X., Xie, L., & Duan, K. (2021). Entrepreneurial ecosystem and the quality and quantity of regional entrepreneurship: A configurational approach. *Journal of Business Research*, *128*, 499–509.

Zbierowski, P. (2012). *Orientacja pozytywna organizacji wysokiej efektywności*. Wolters Kluwer Polska.

Index

Note: **Bold** page numbers refer to tables and *italic* page numbers refer to figures.

For Product Safety Concerns and Information please contact our EU representative GPSR@taylorandfrancis.com Taylor & Francis Verlag GmbH, Kaufingerstraße 24, 80331 München, Germany